Printed in the United States of America

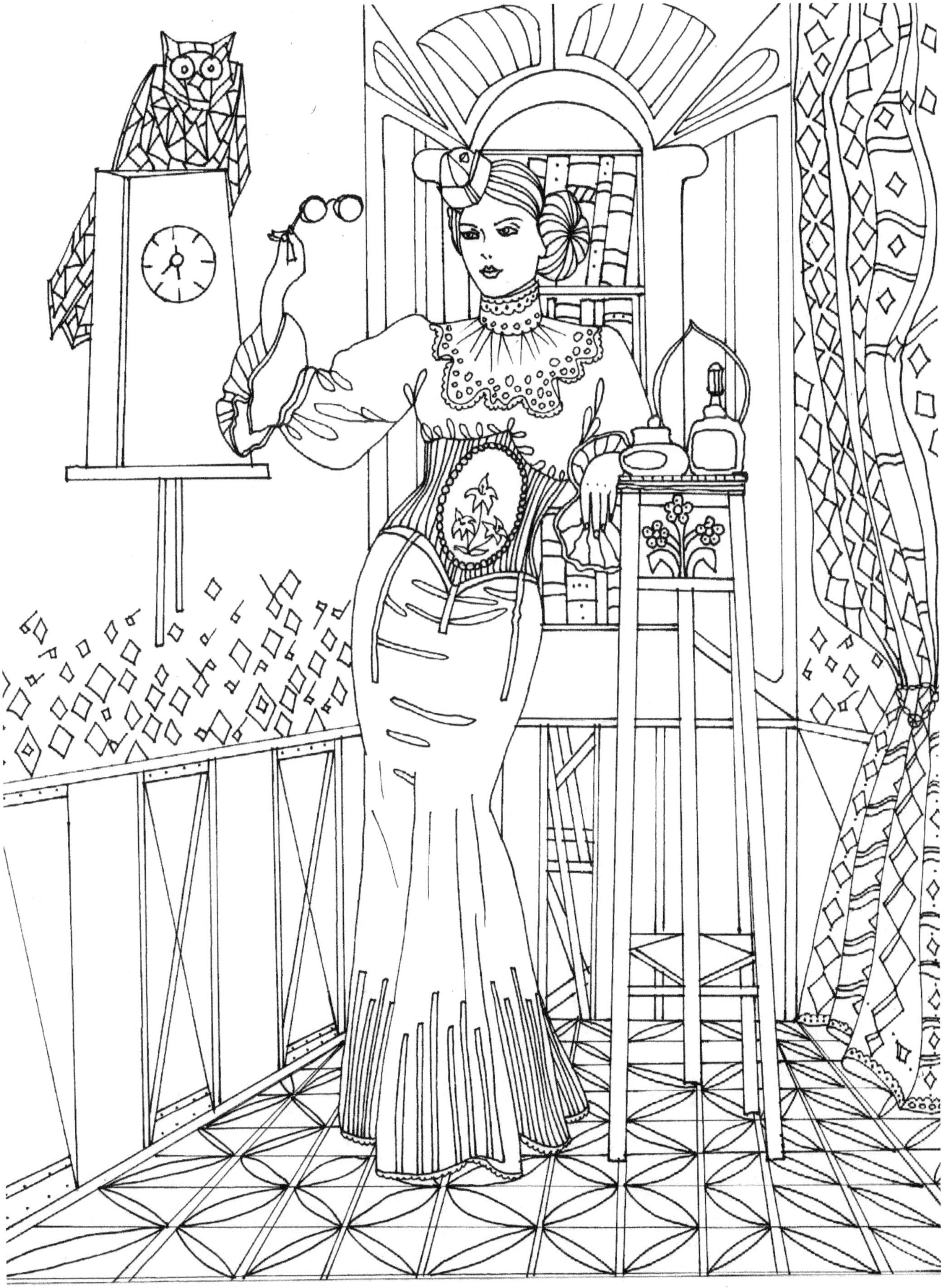

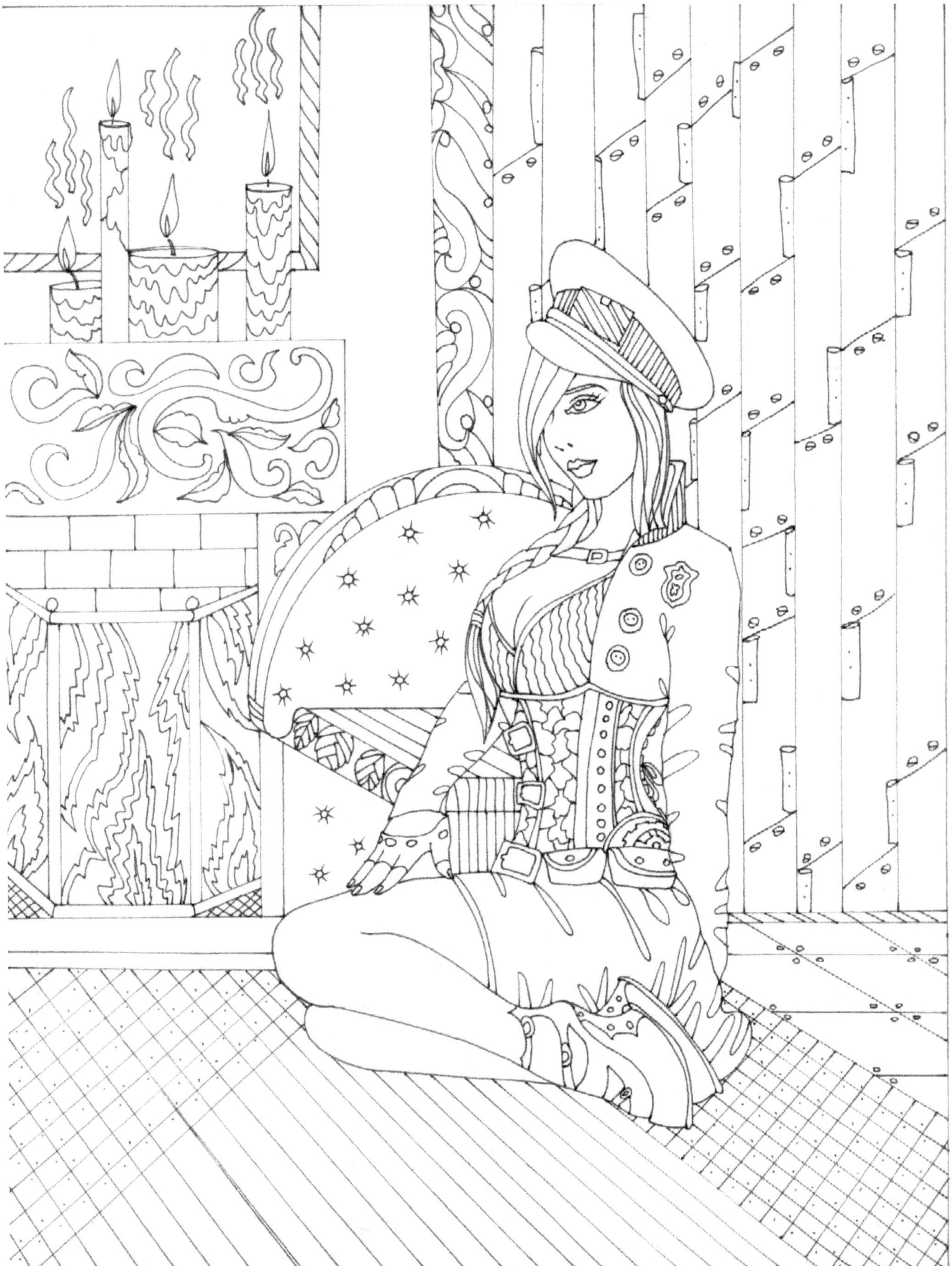

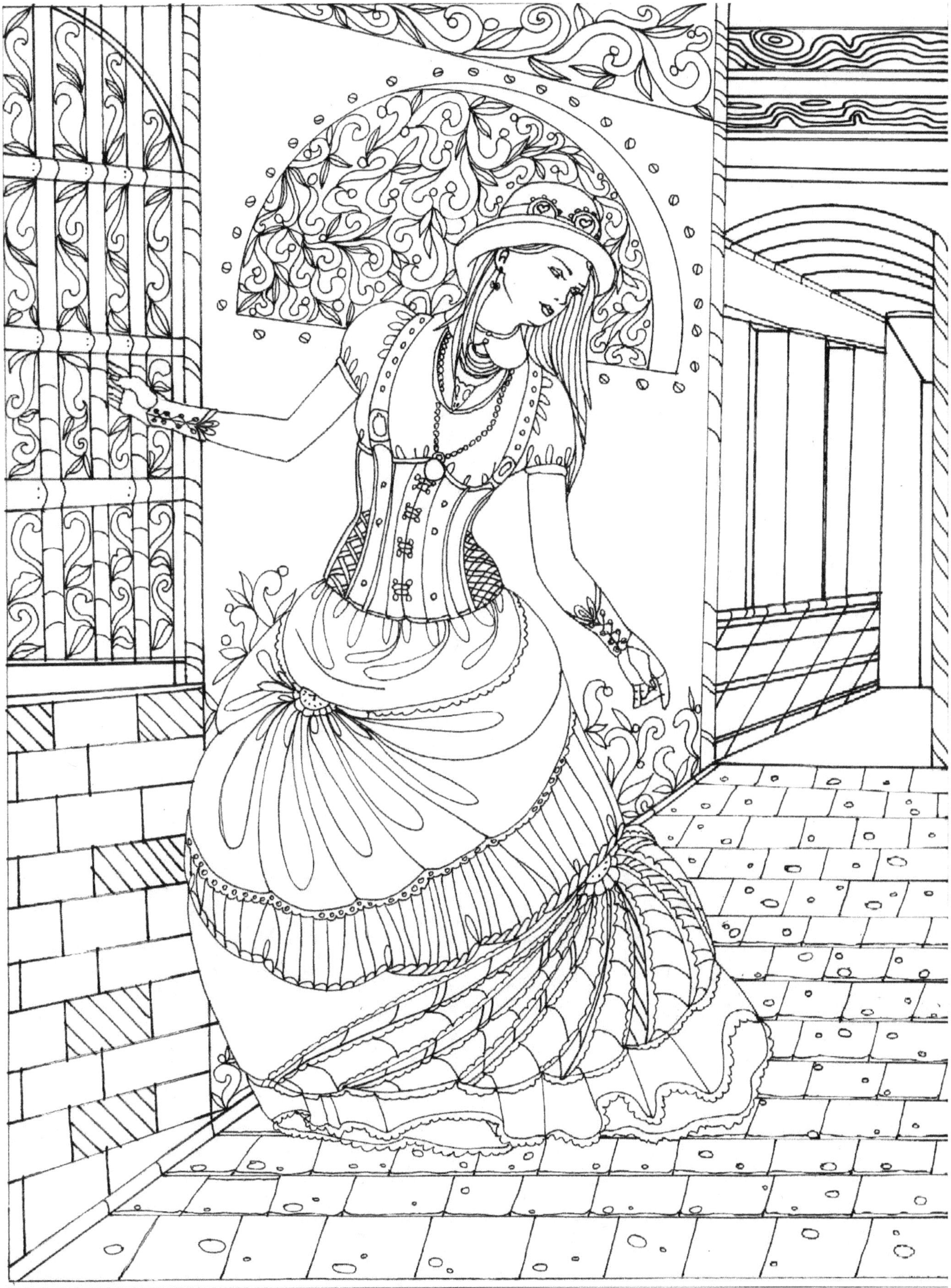

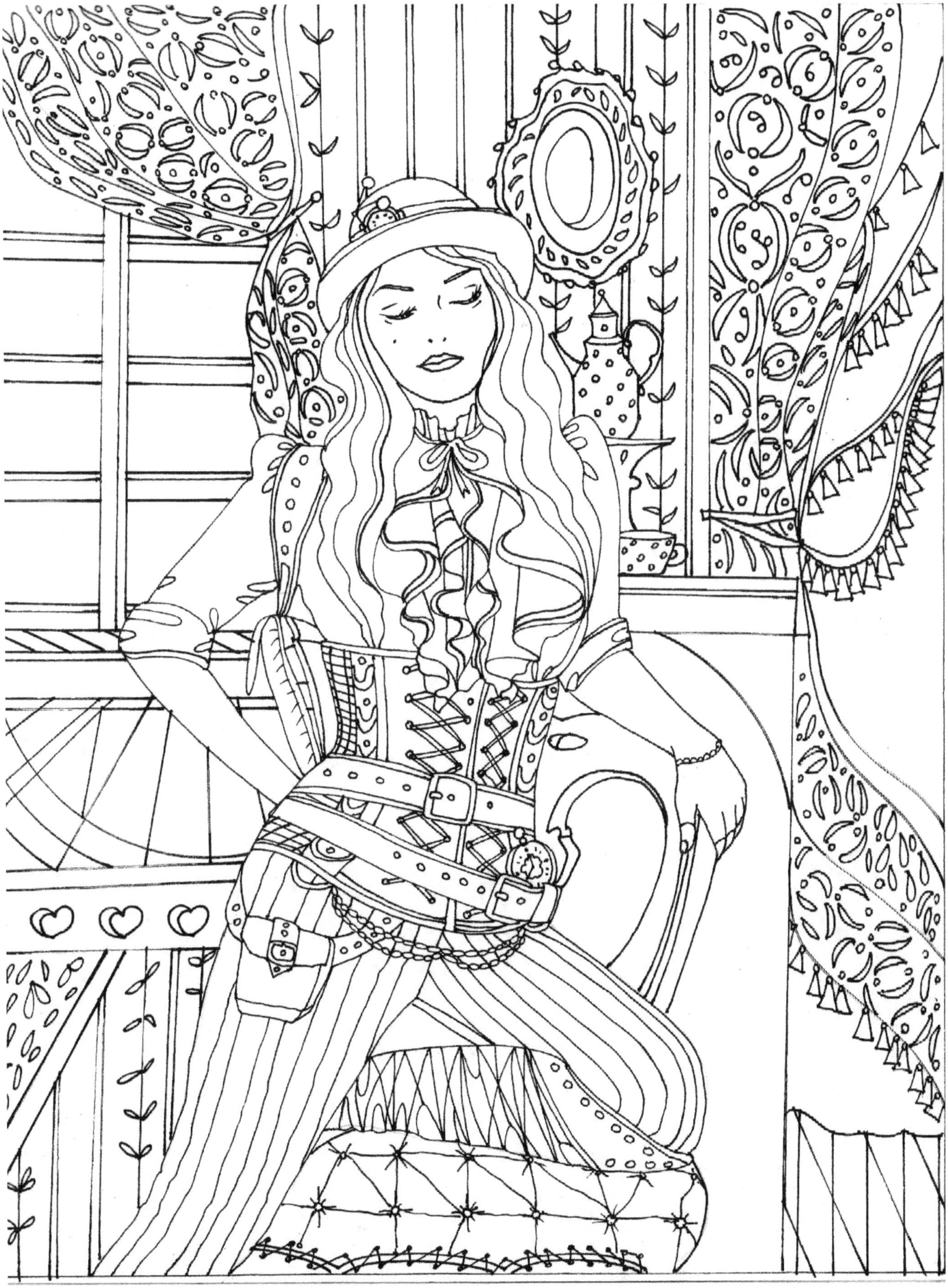

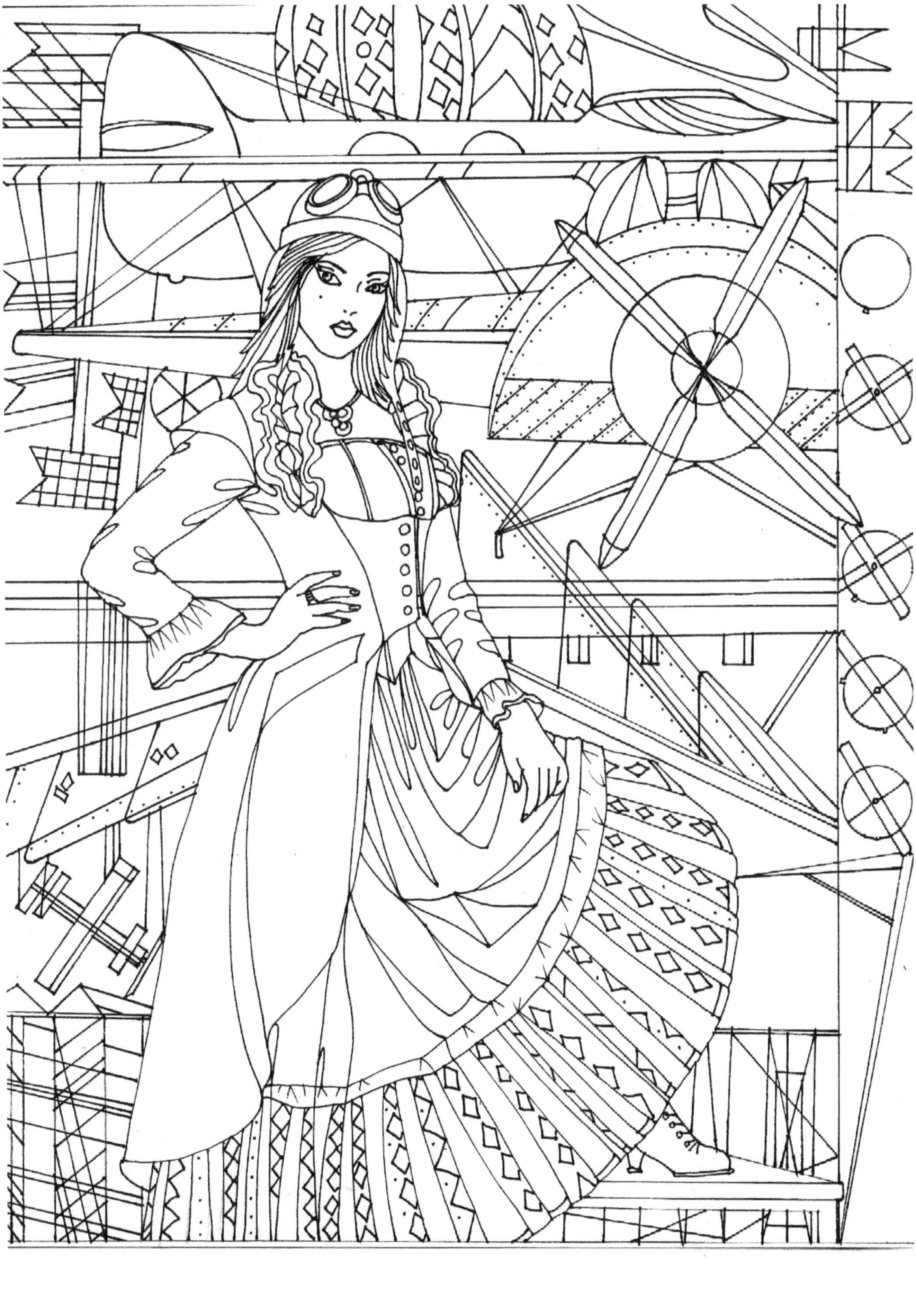

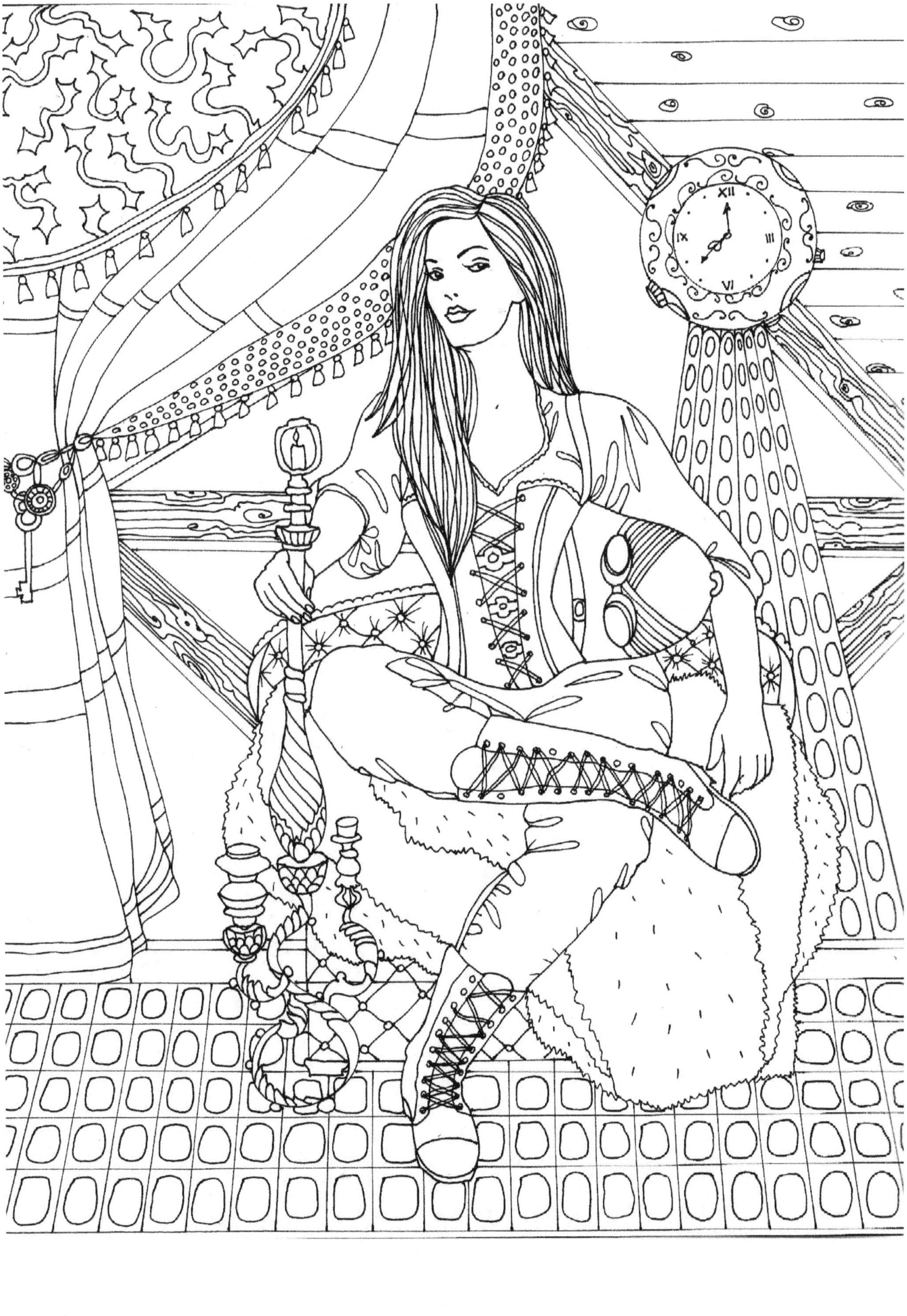
XII
III
VI
IX

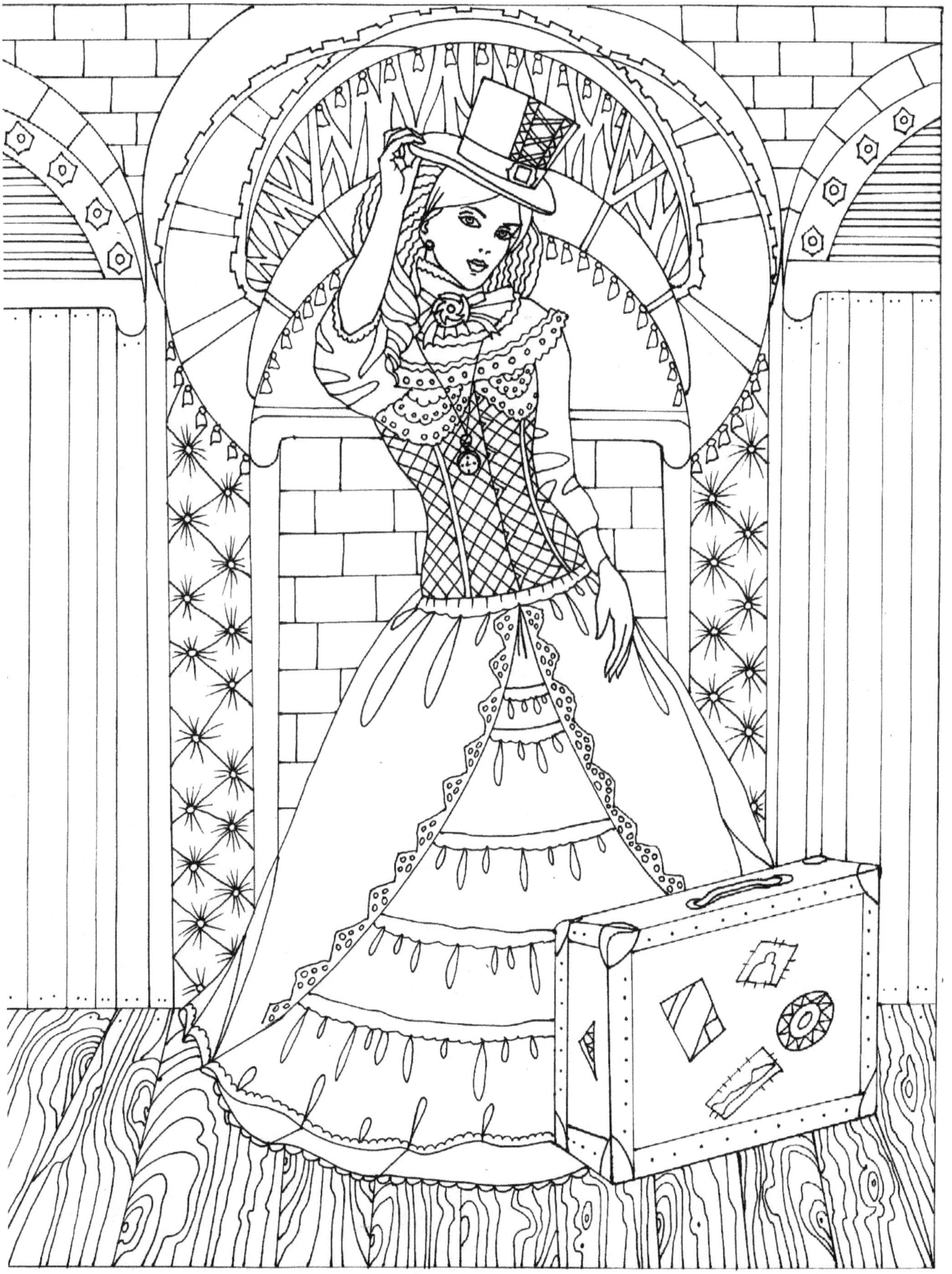

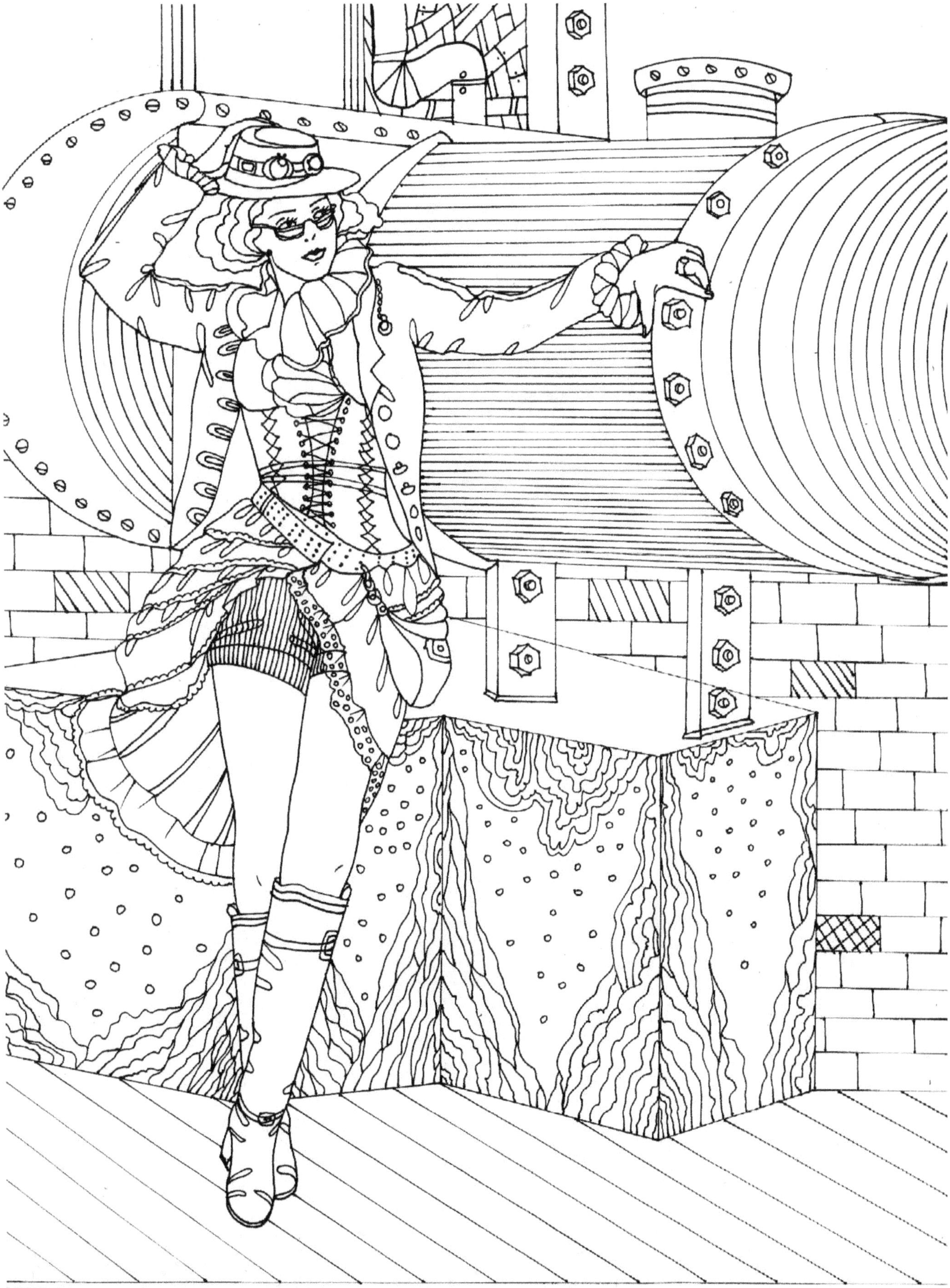

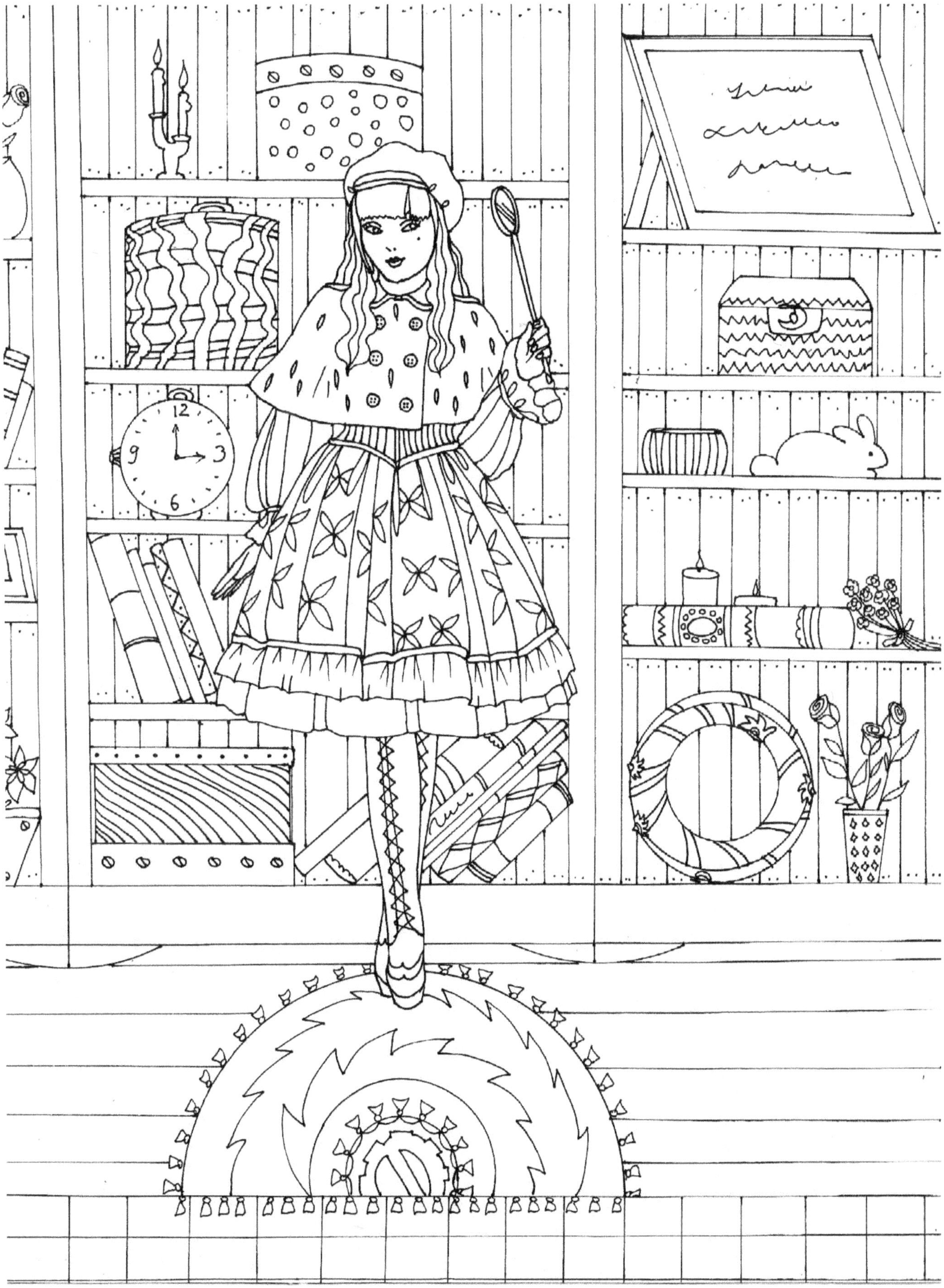
12
9
3
6

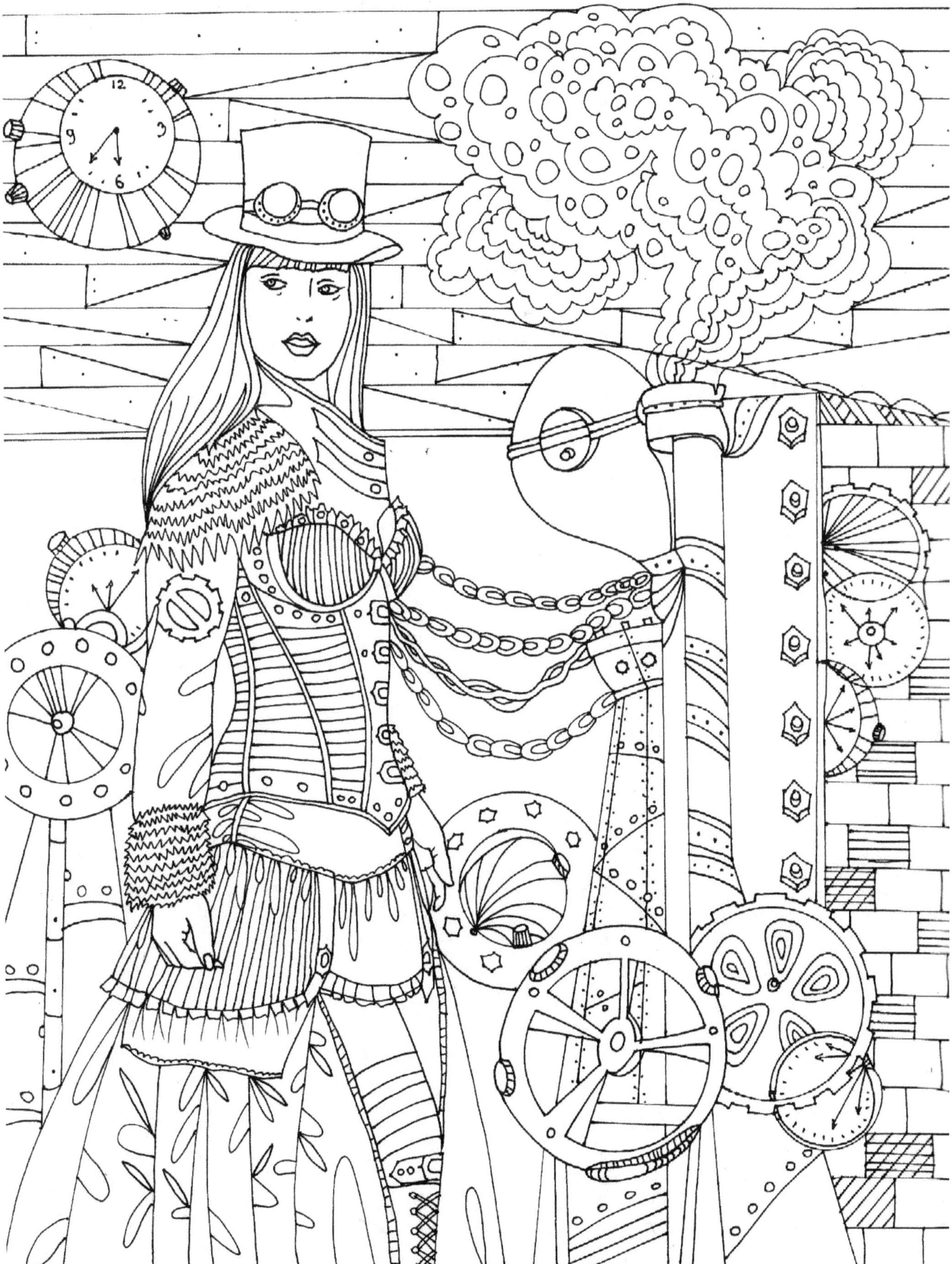

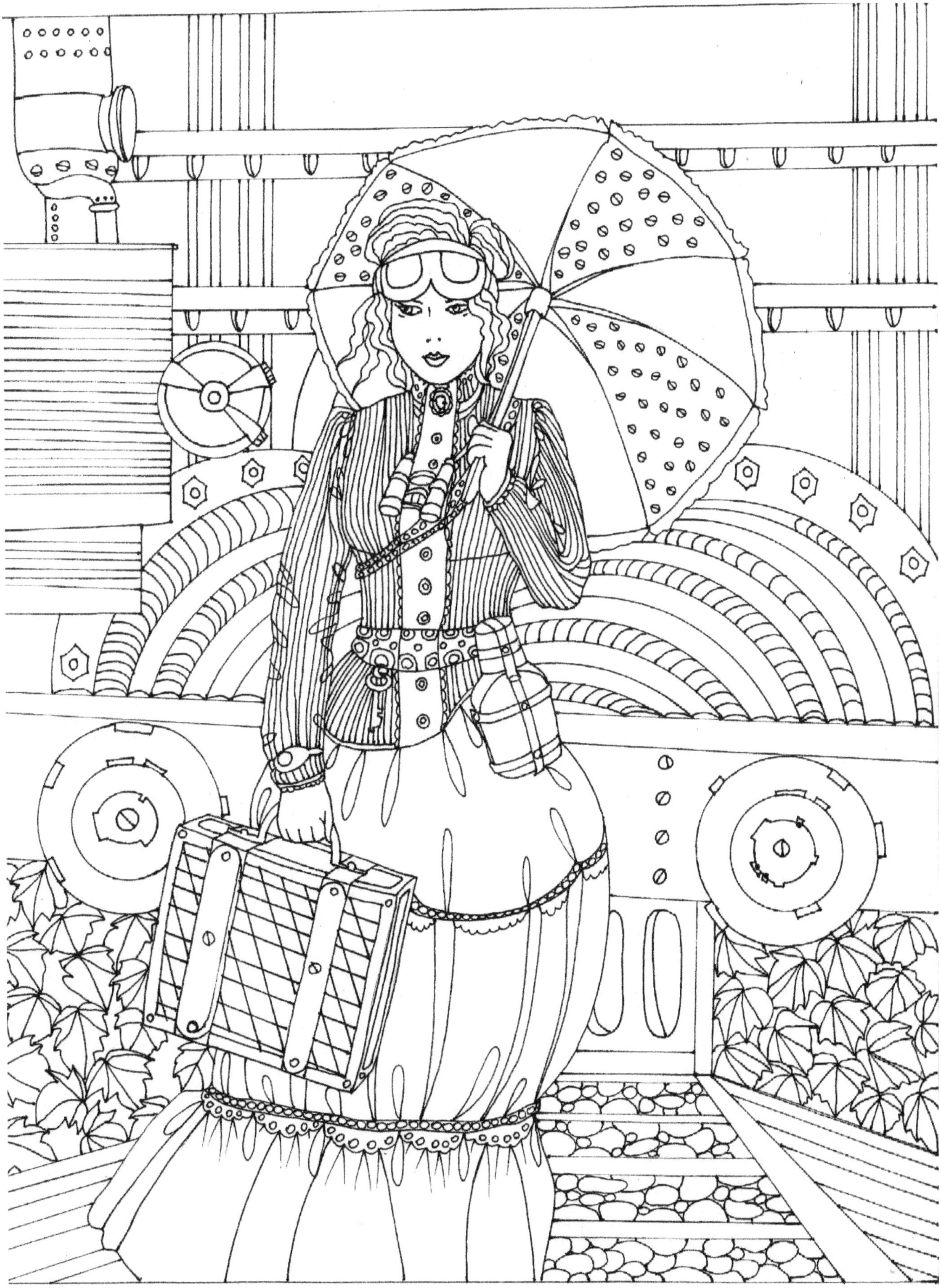

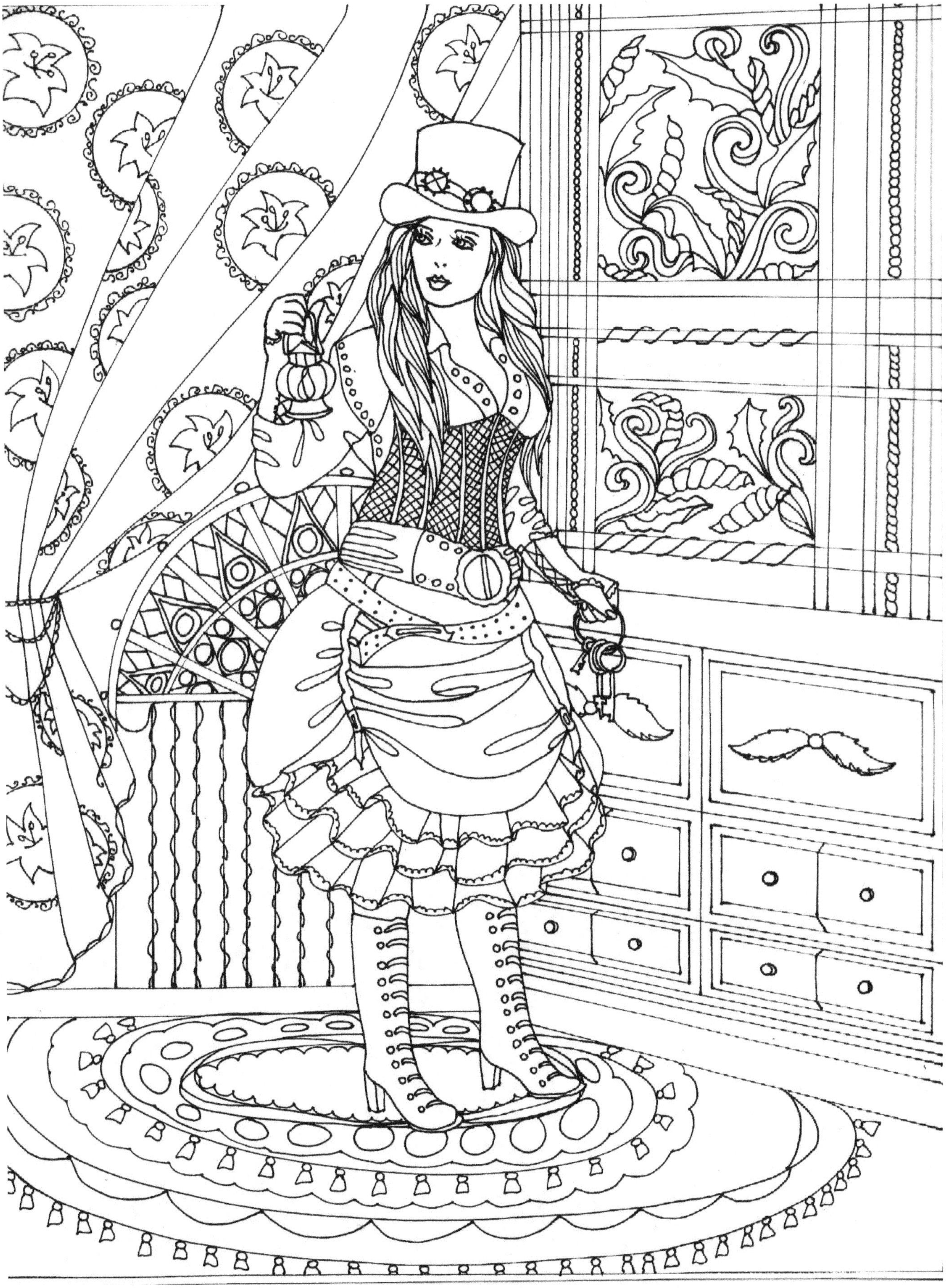

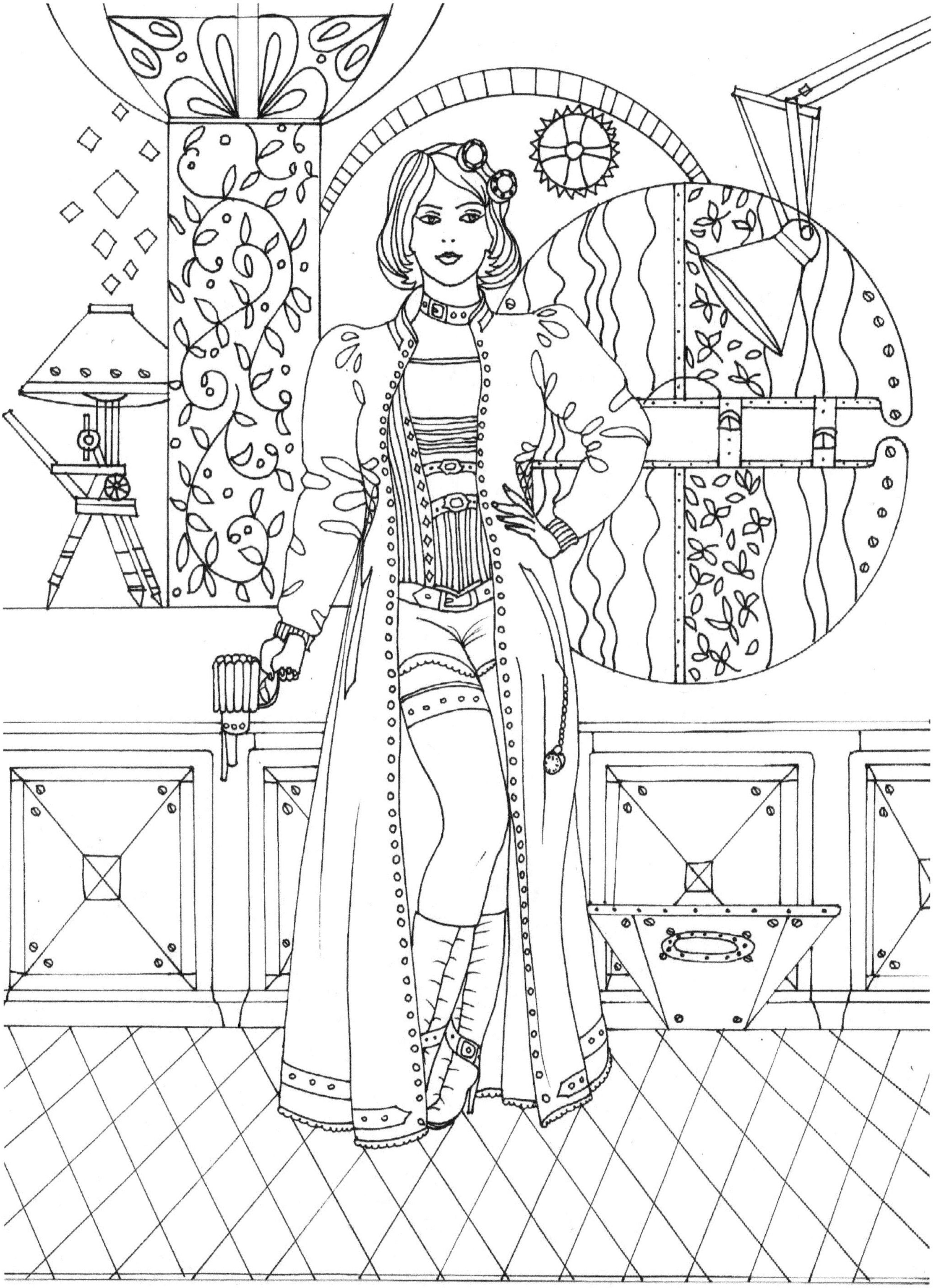

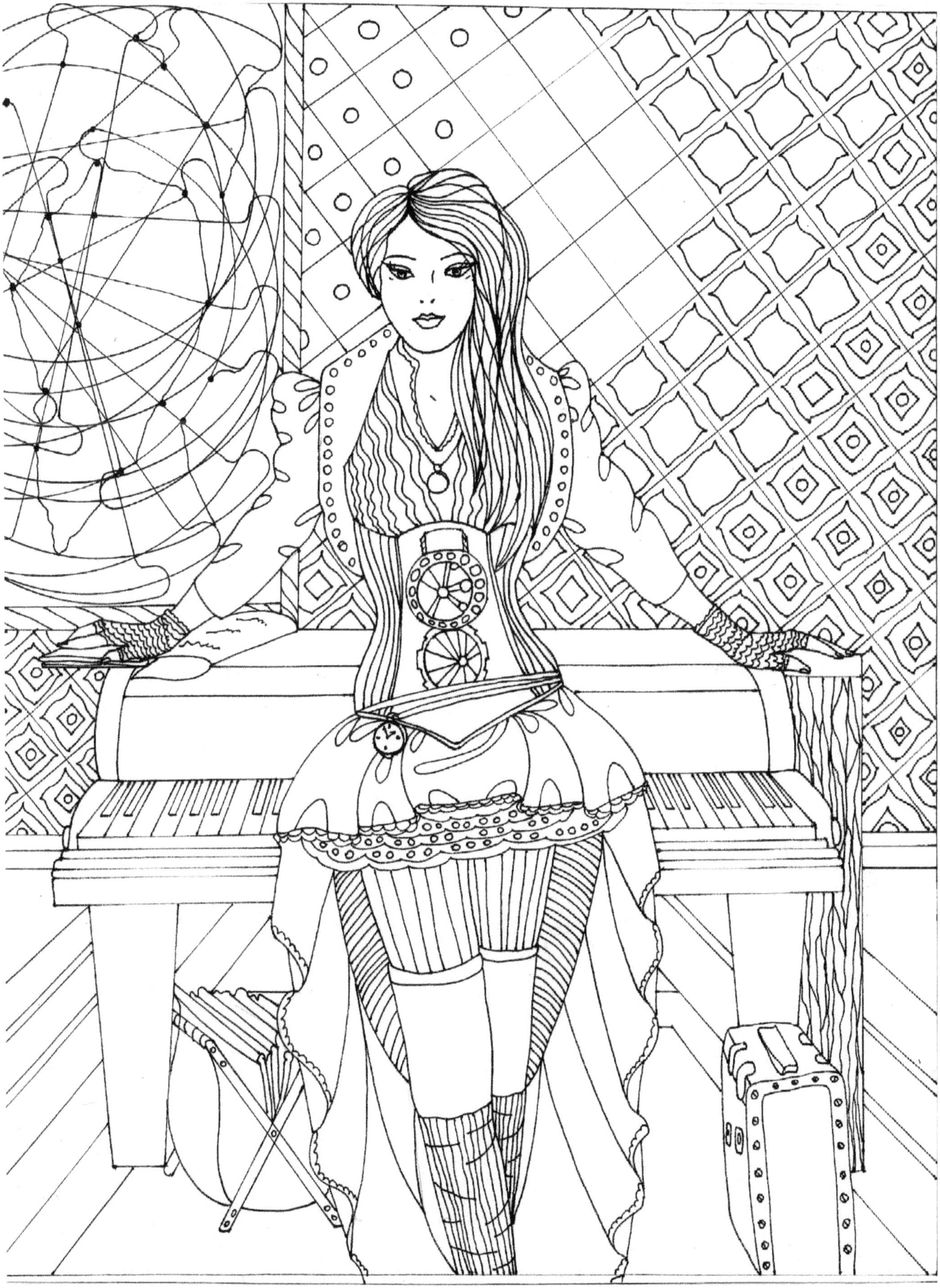

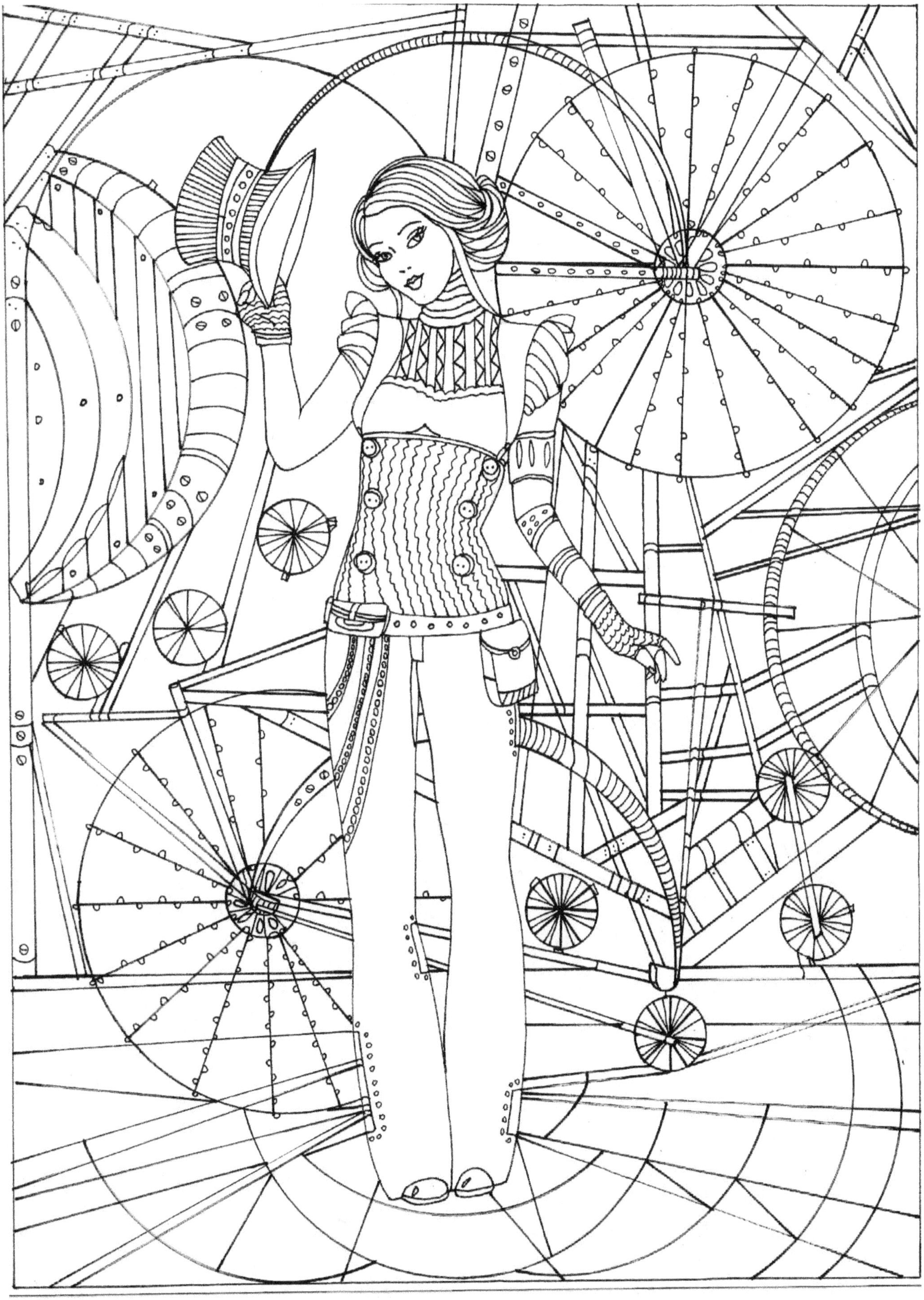

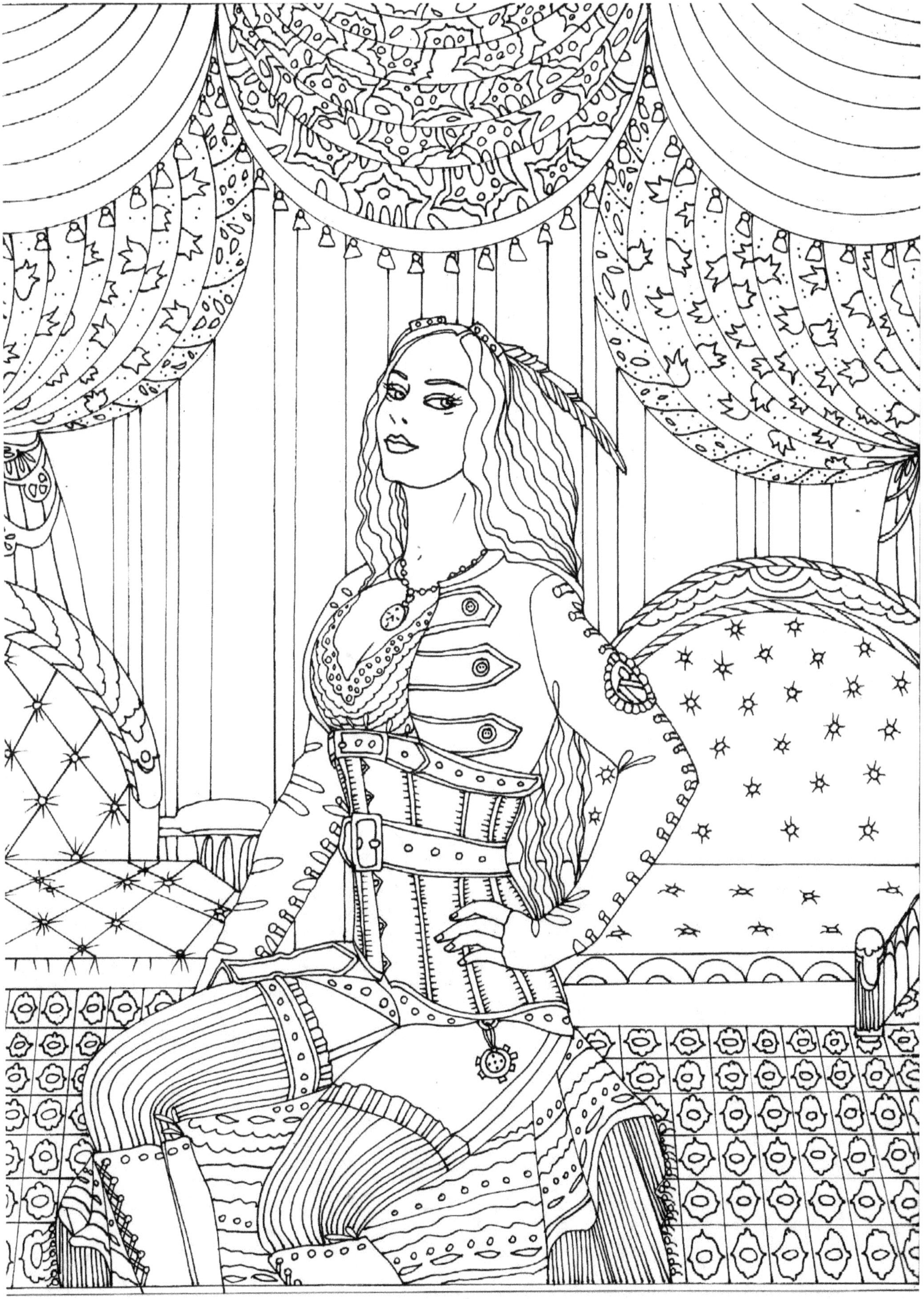

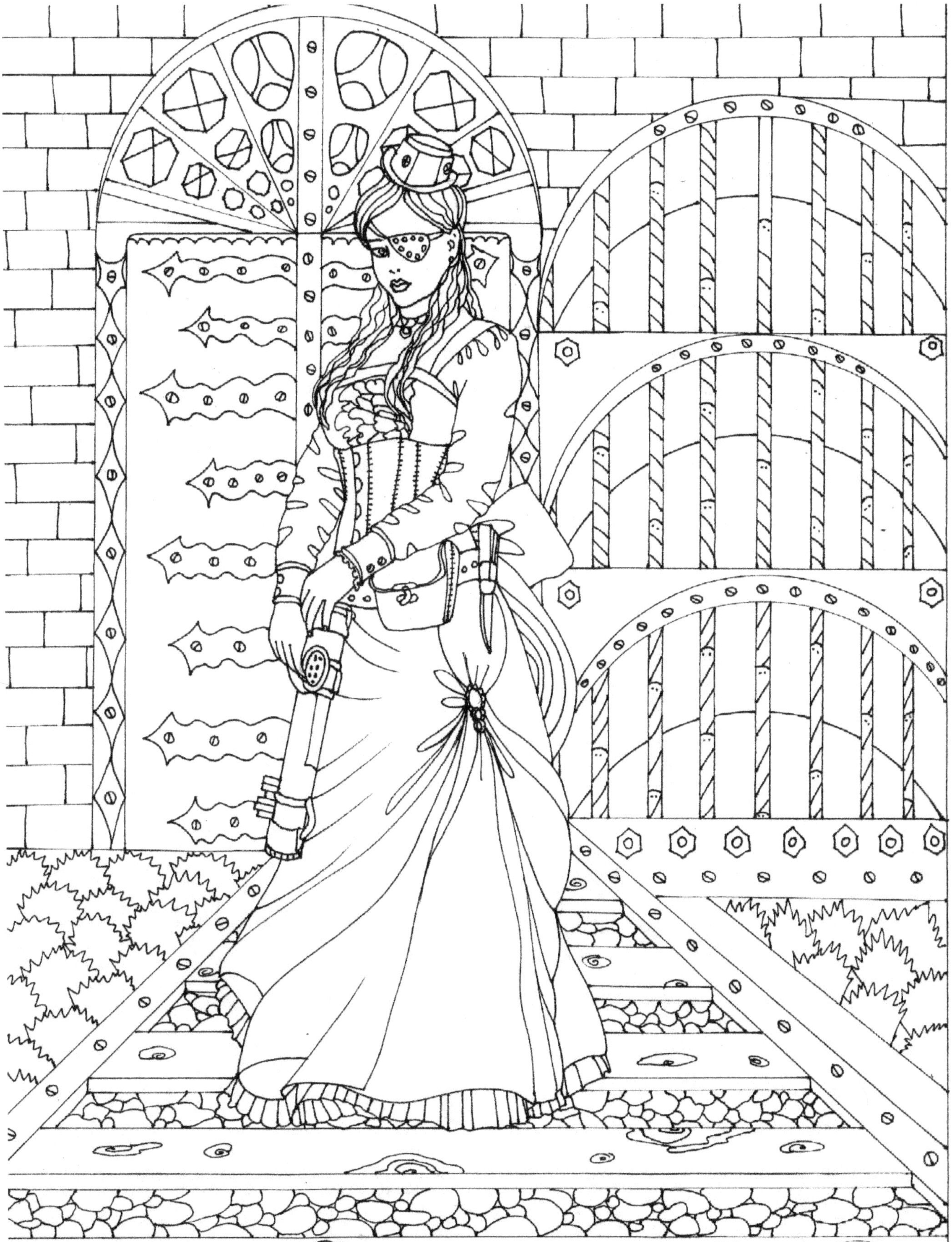

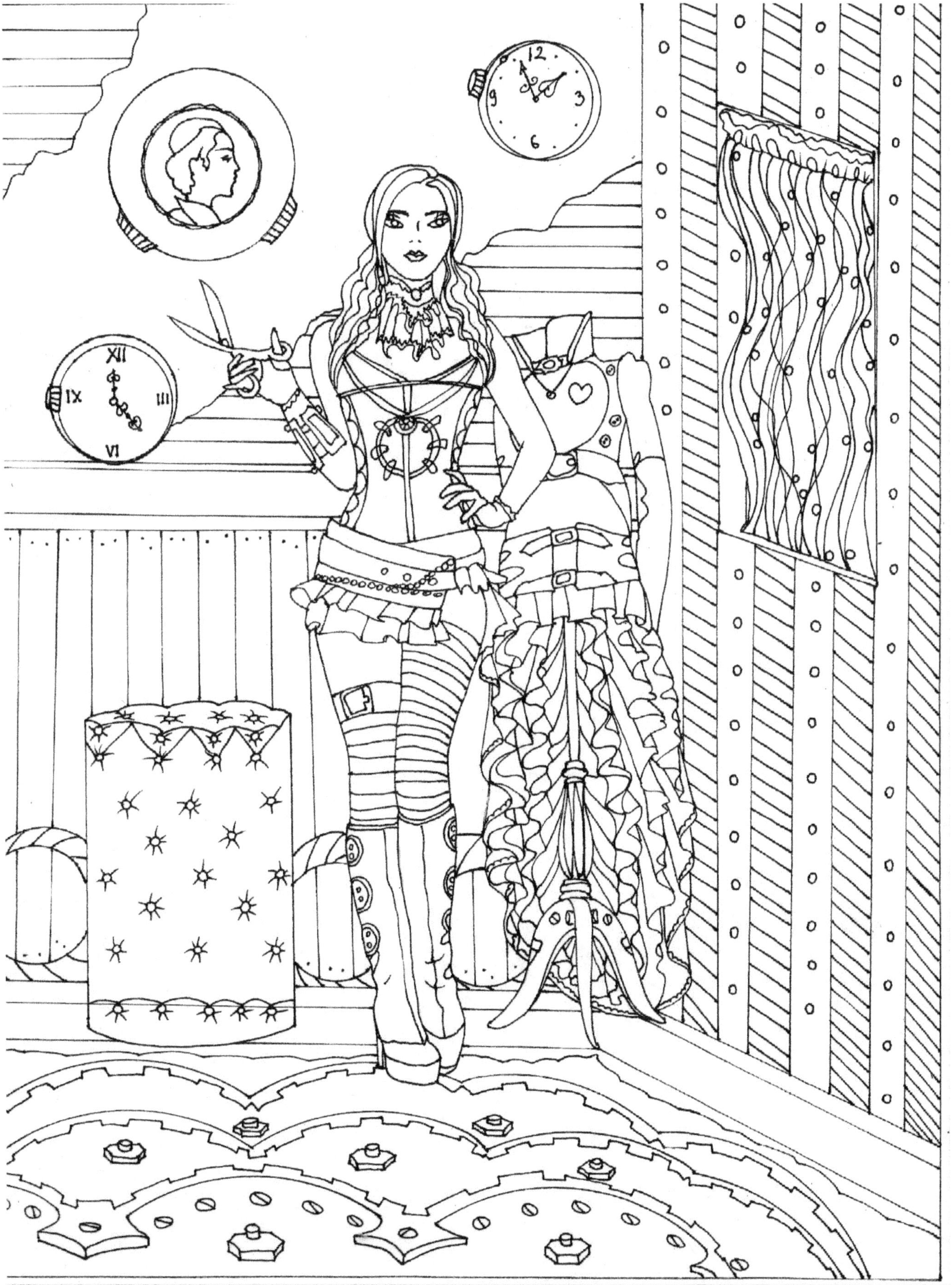
XII
IX
III
VI
12
9
3
6

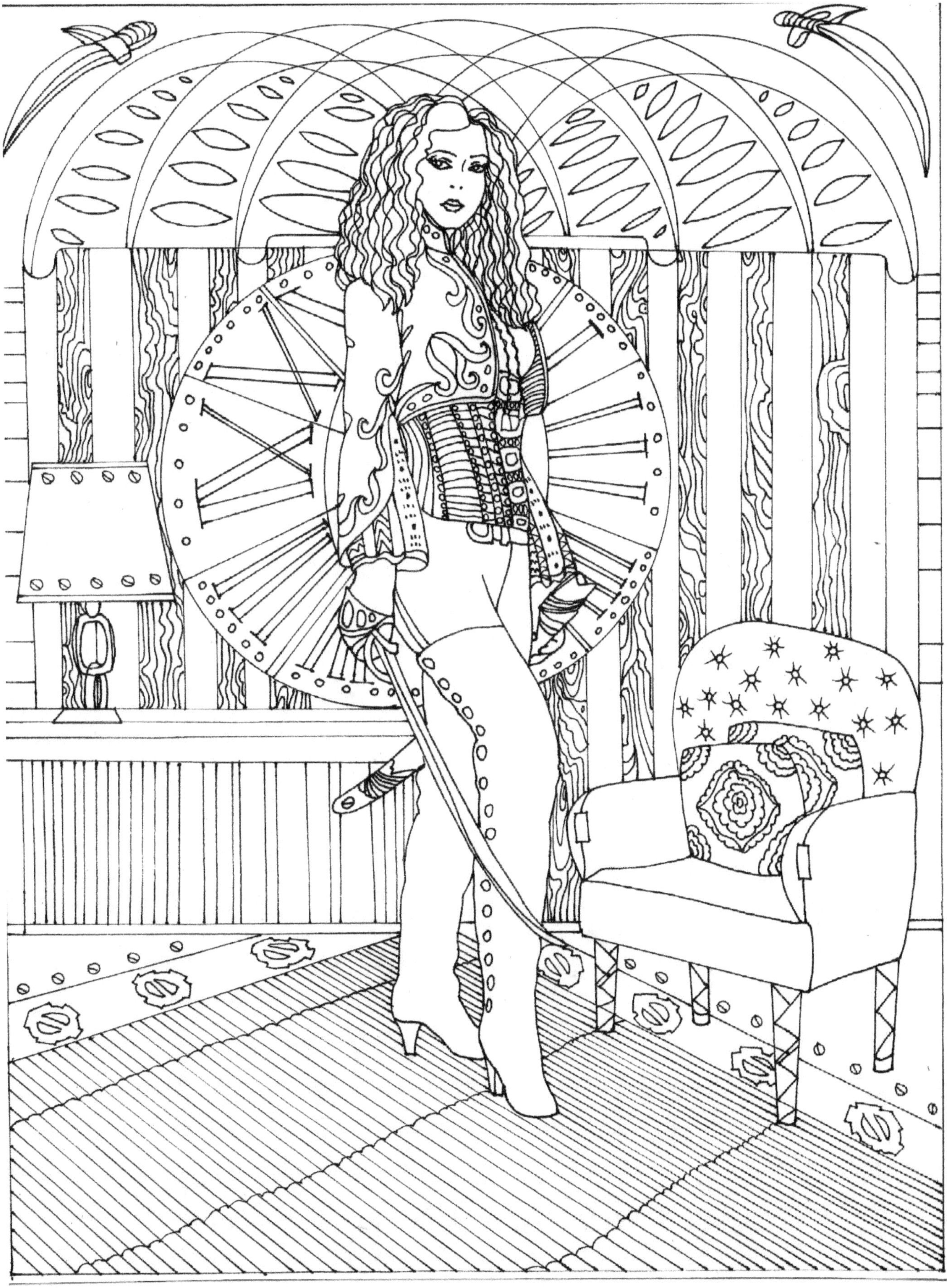

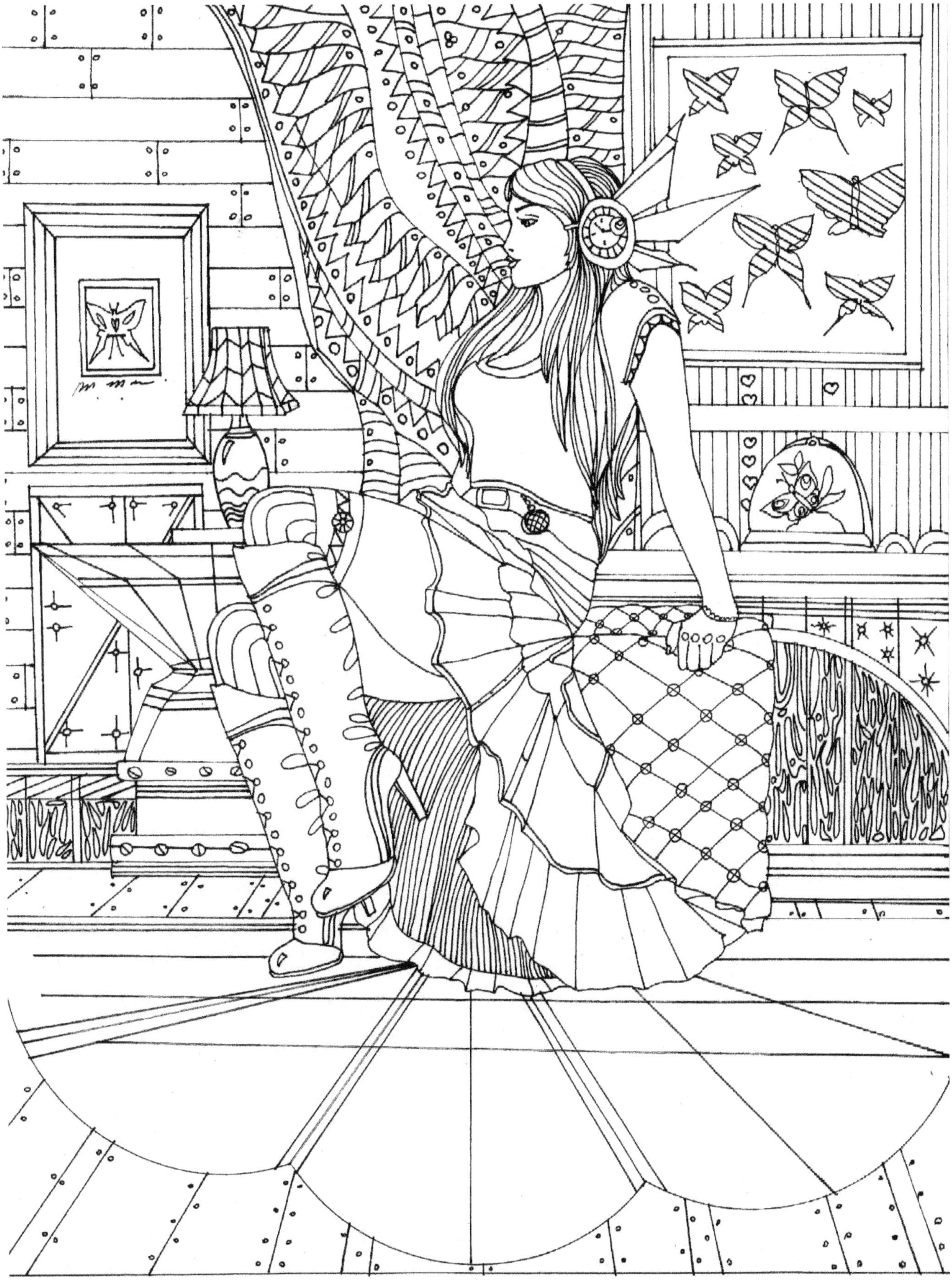

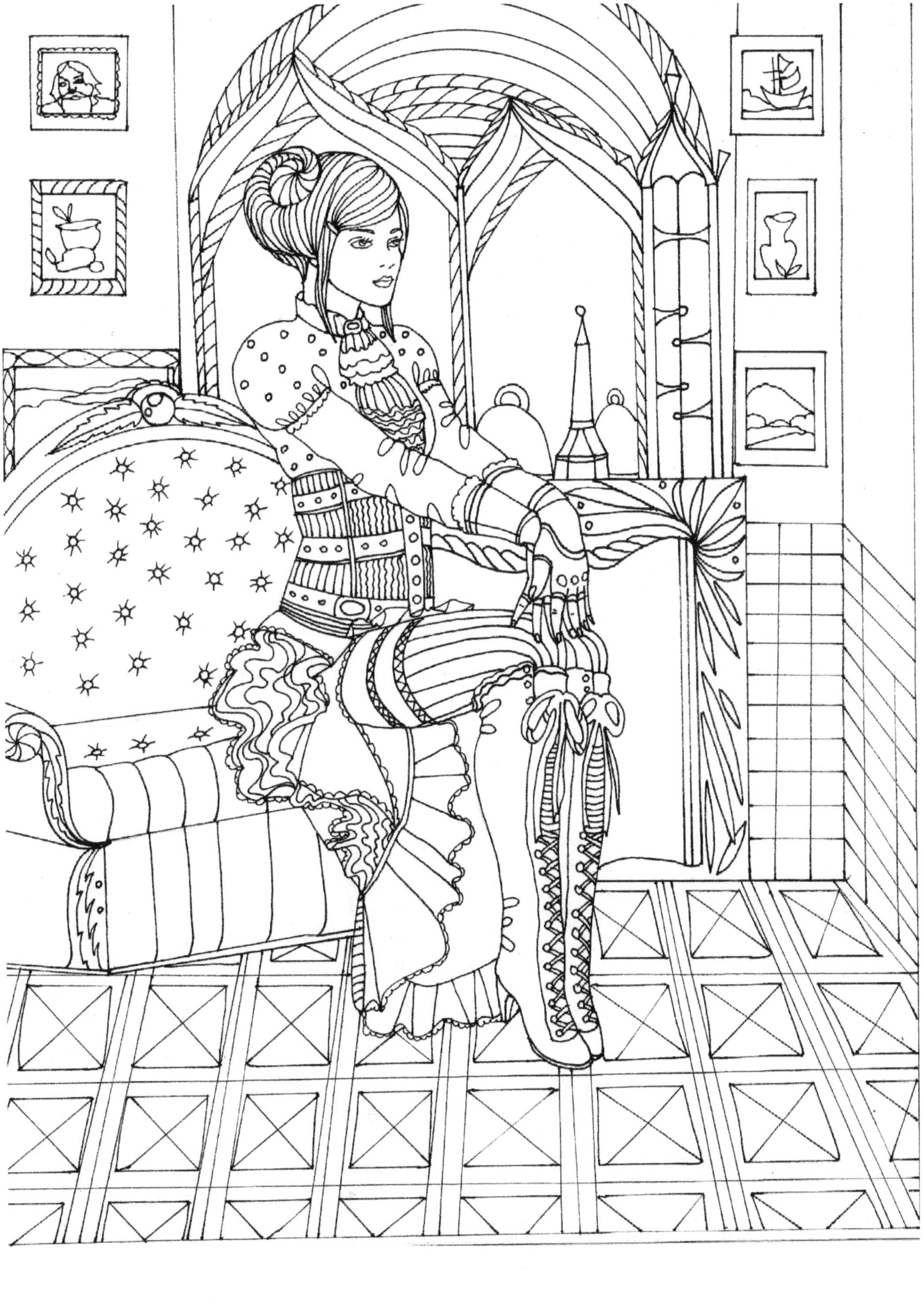

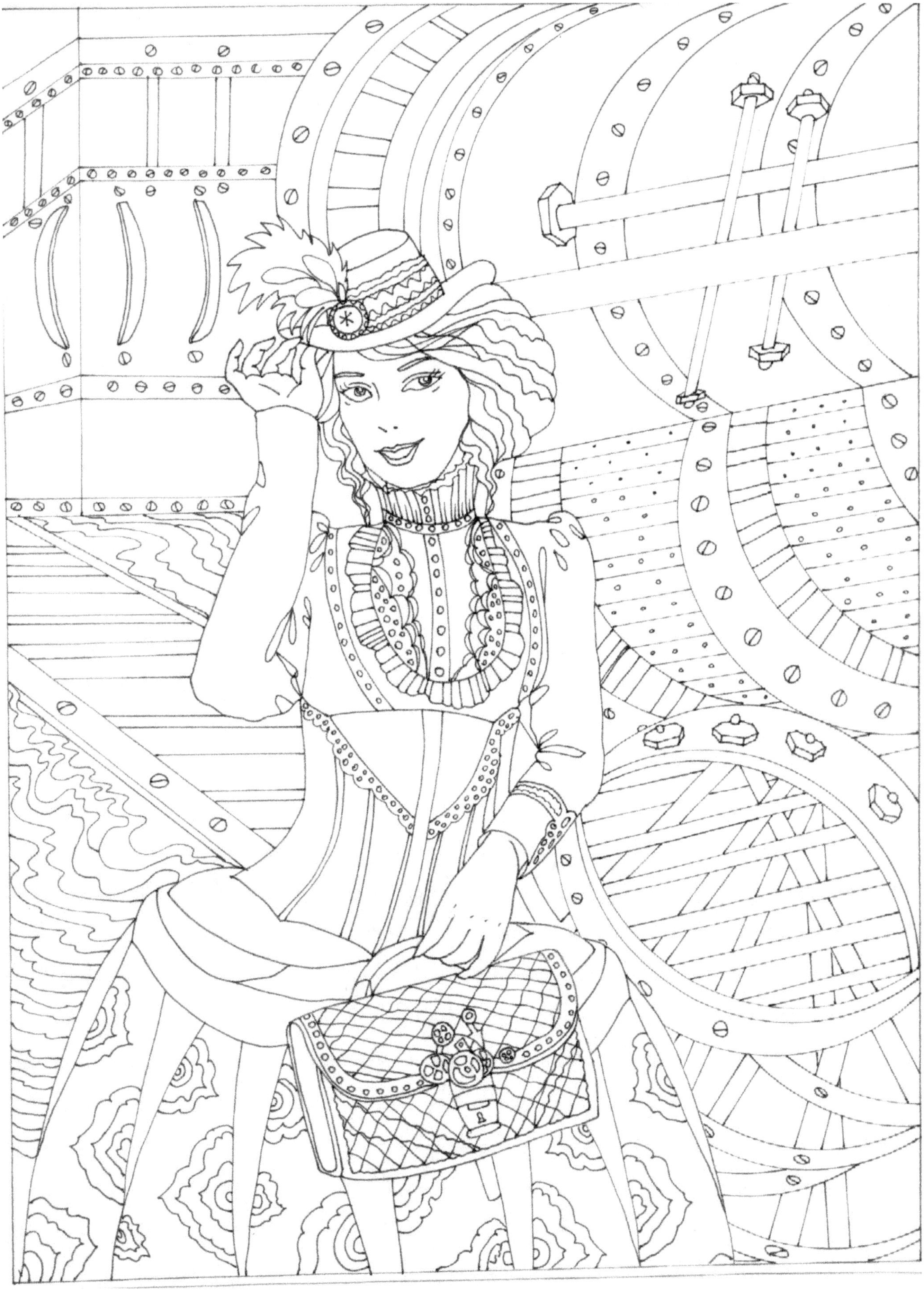

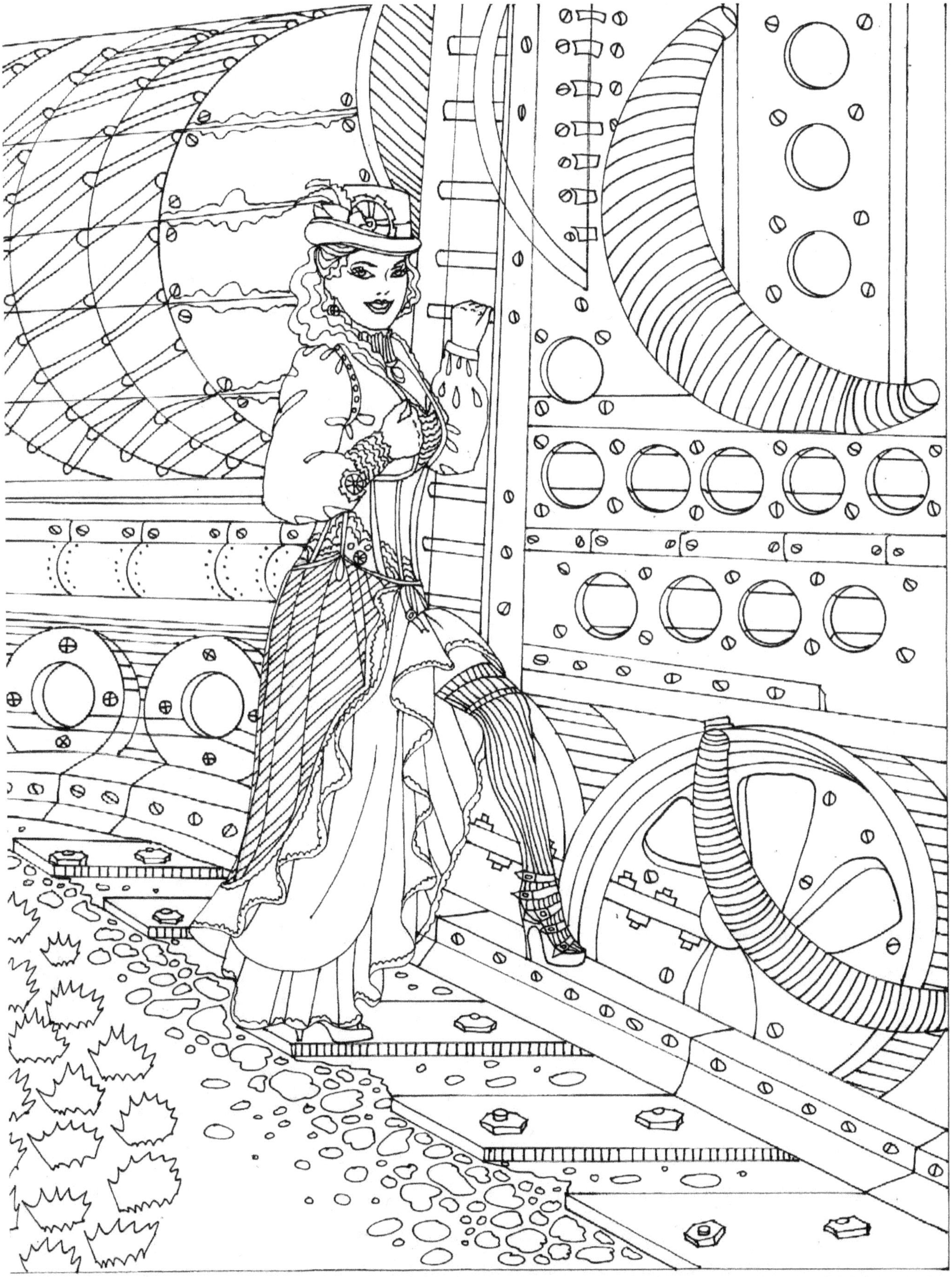

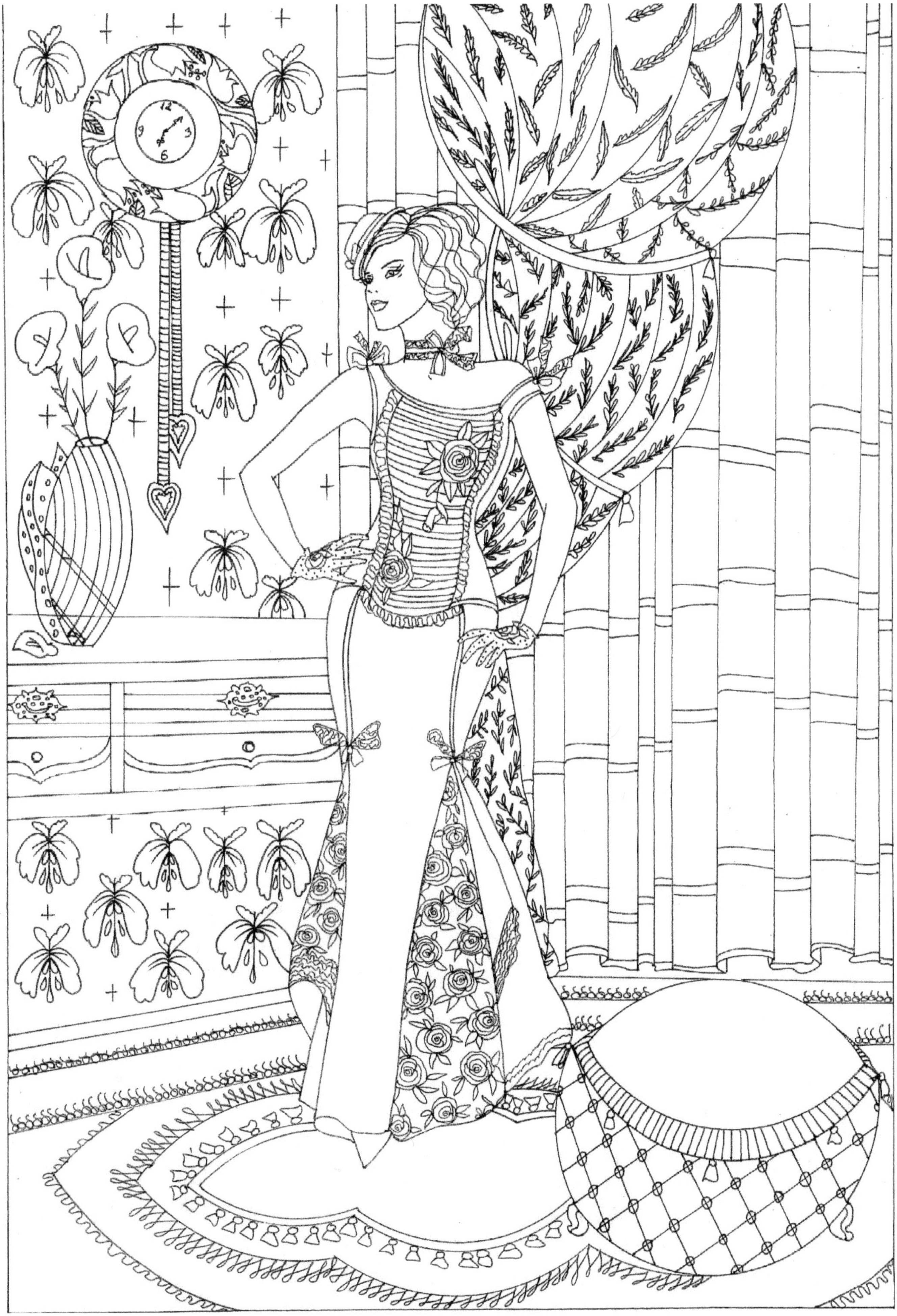

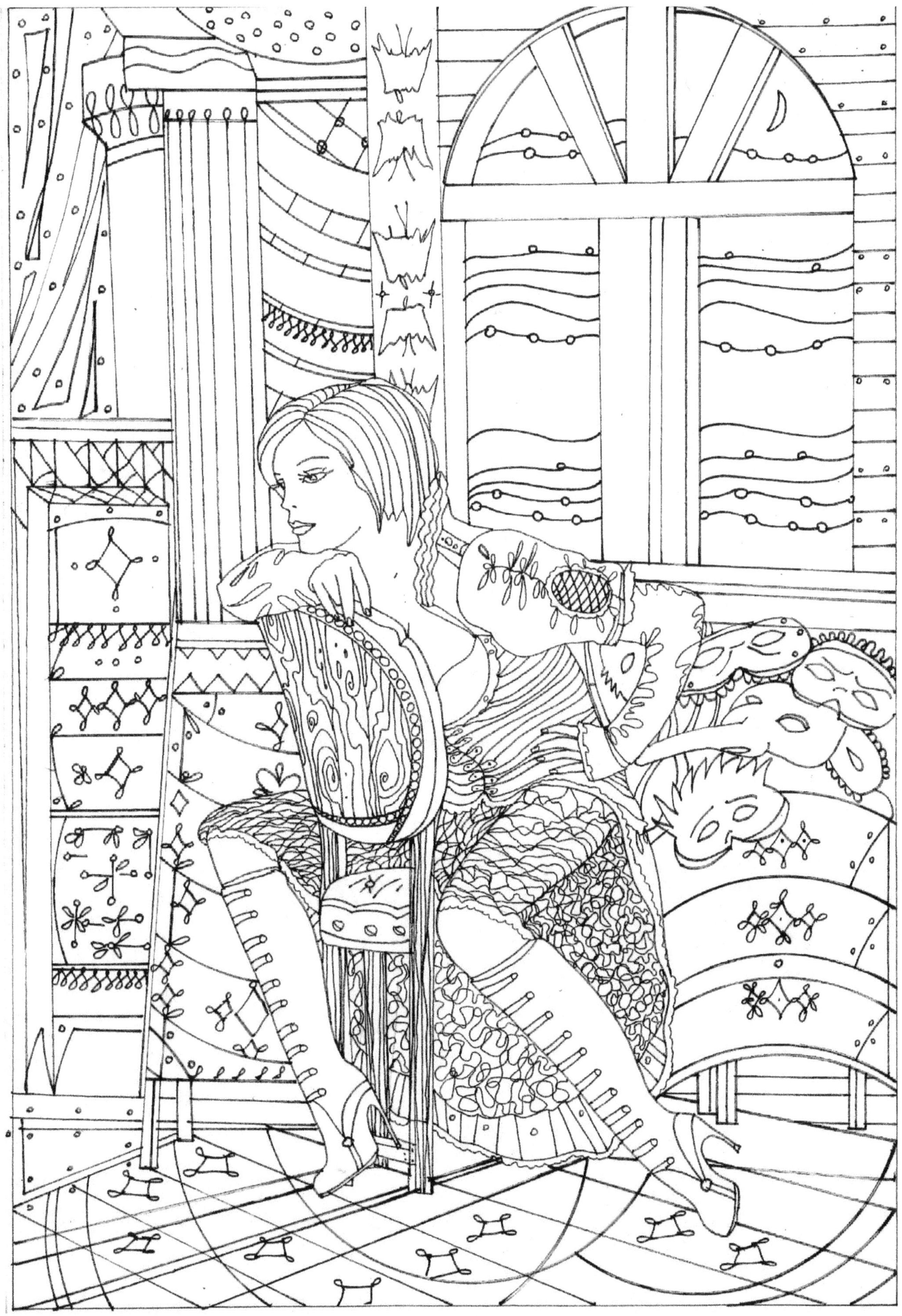

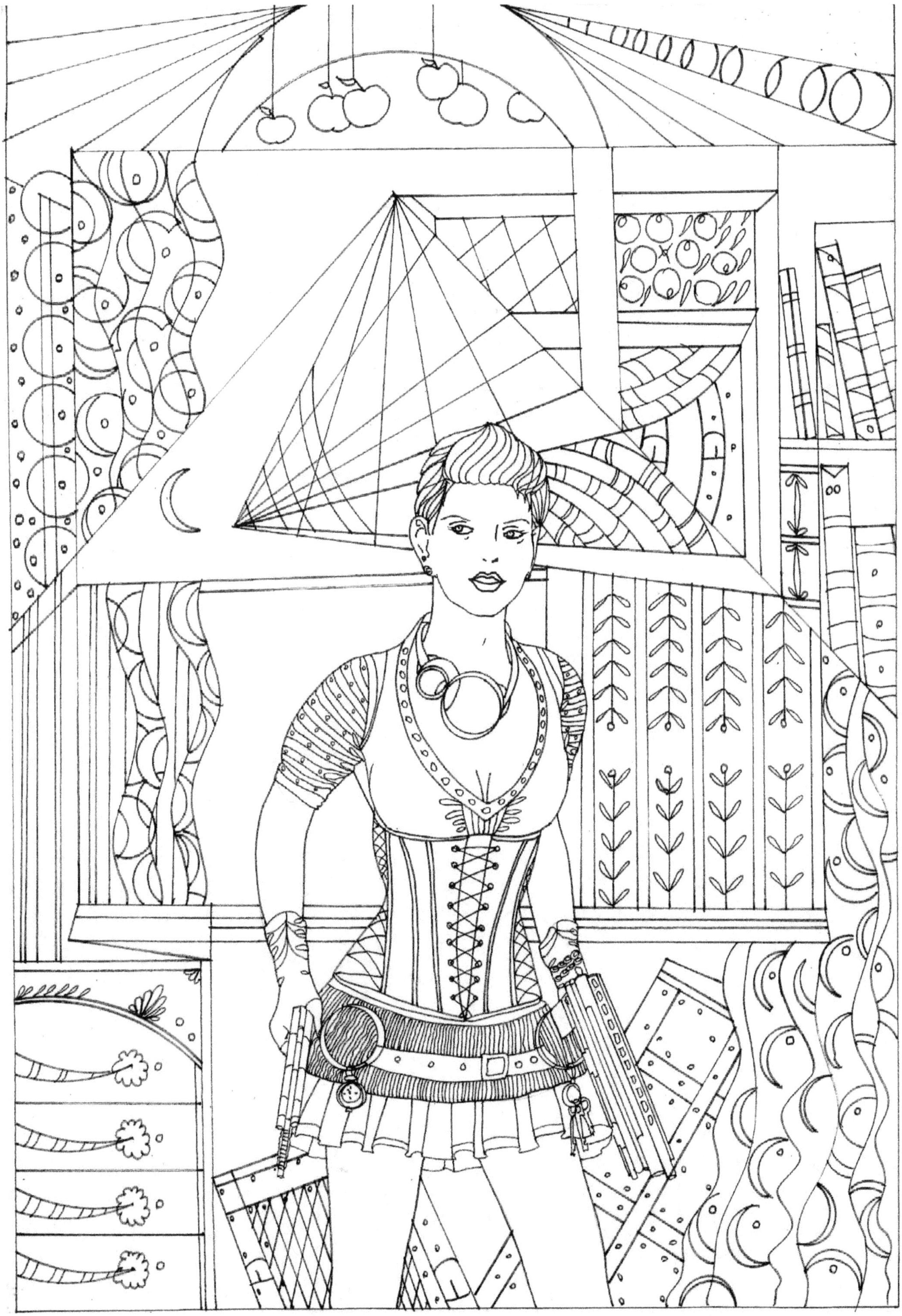

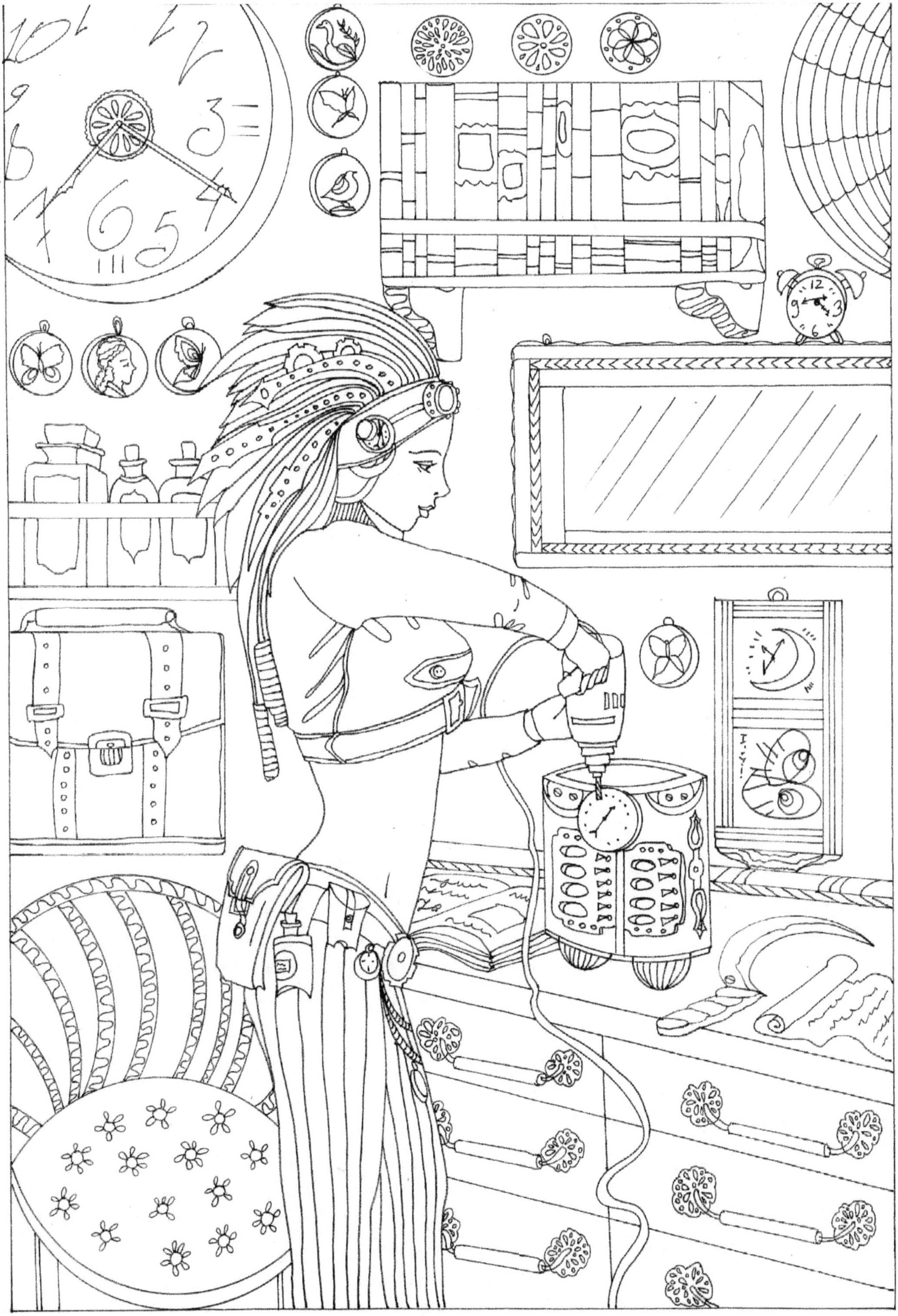

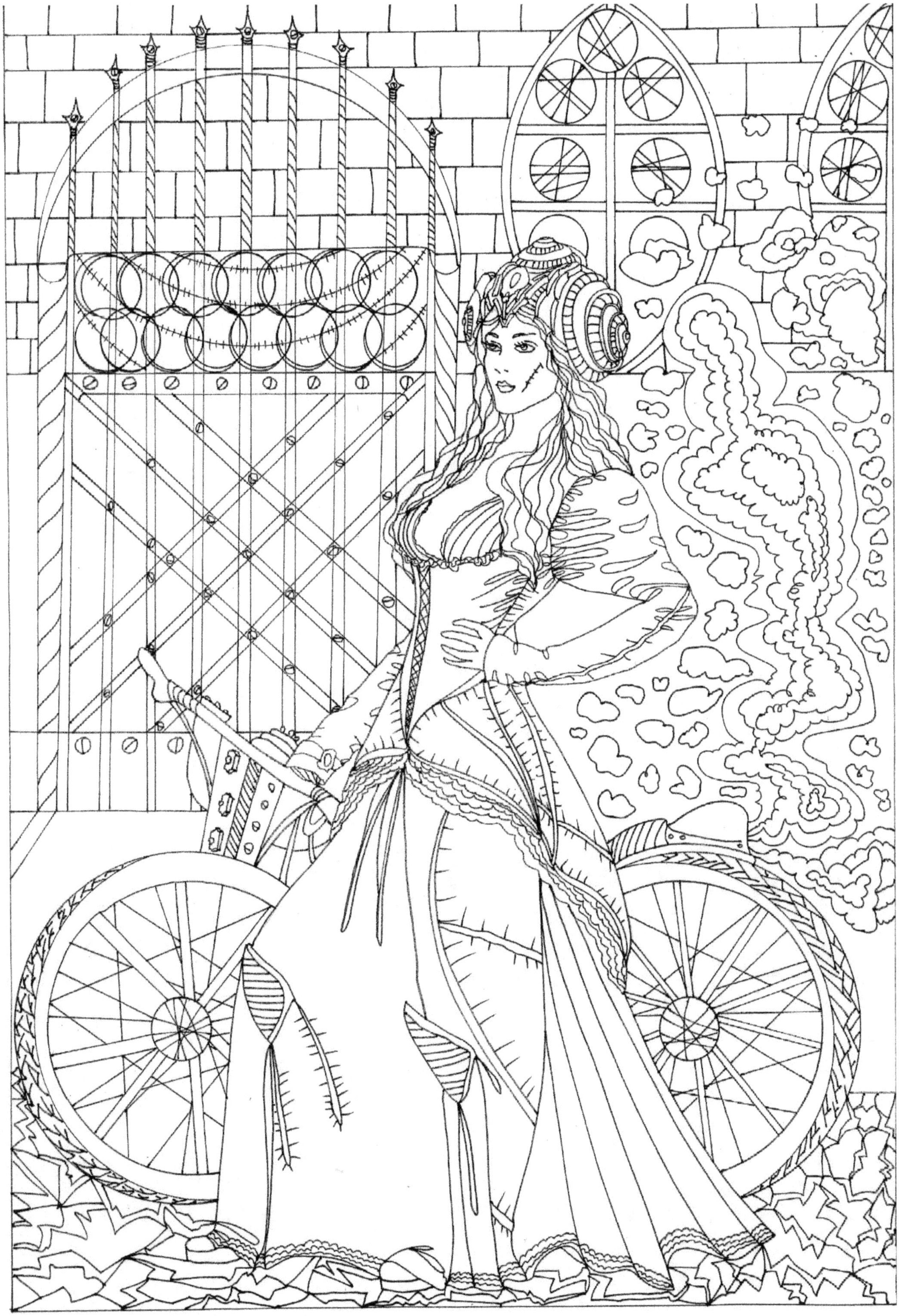

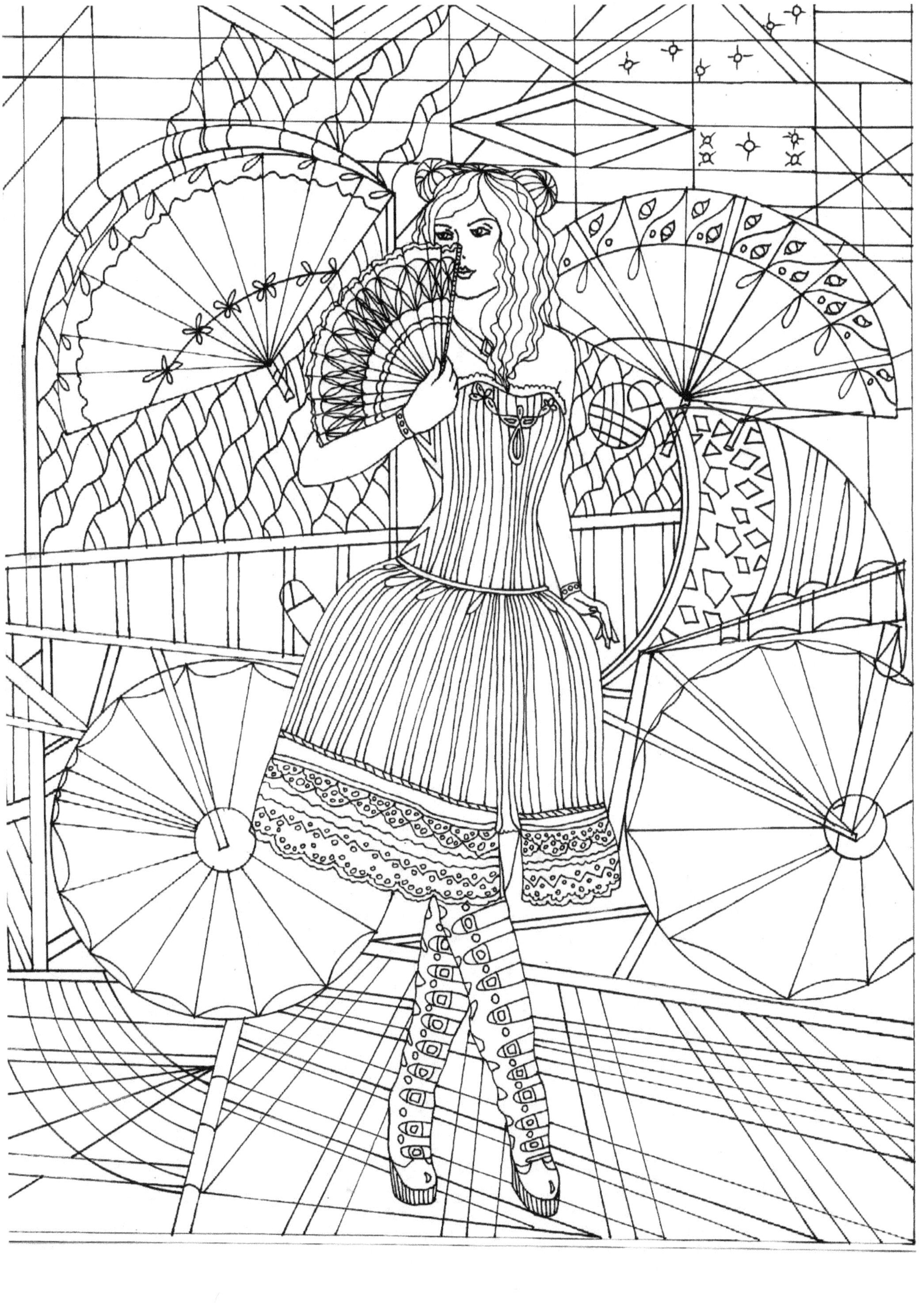

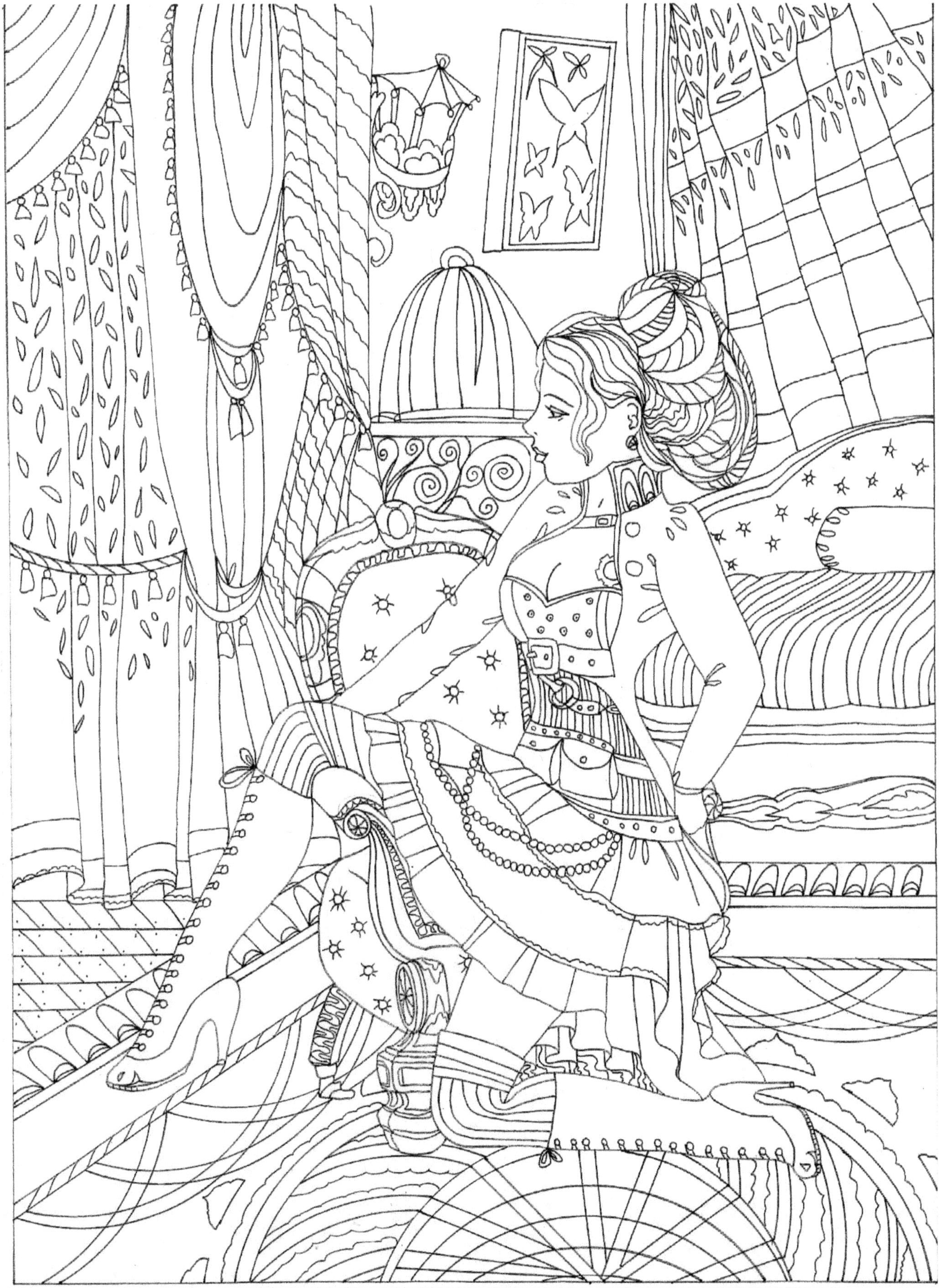

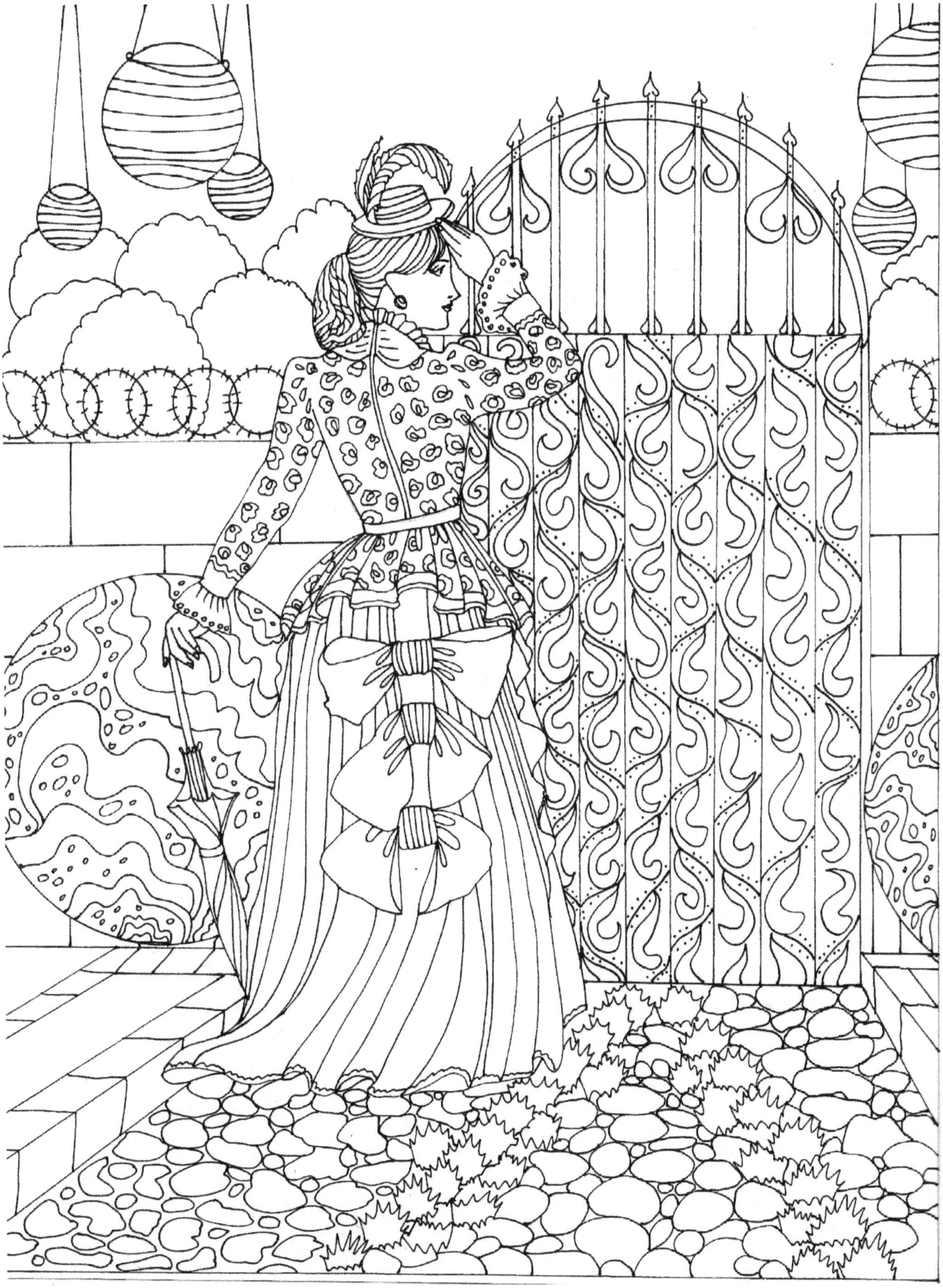

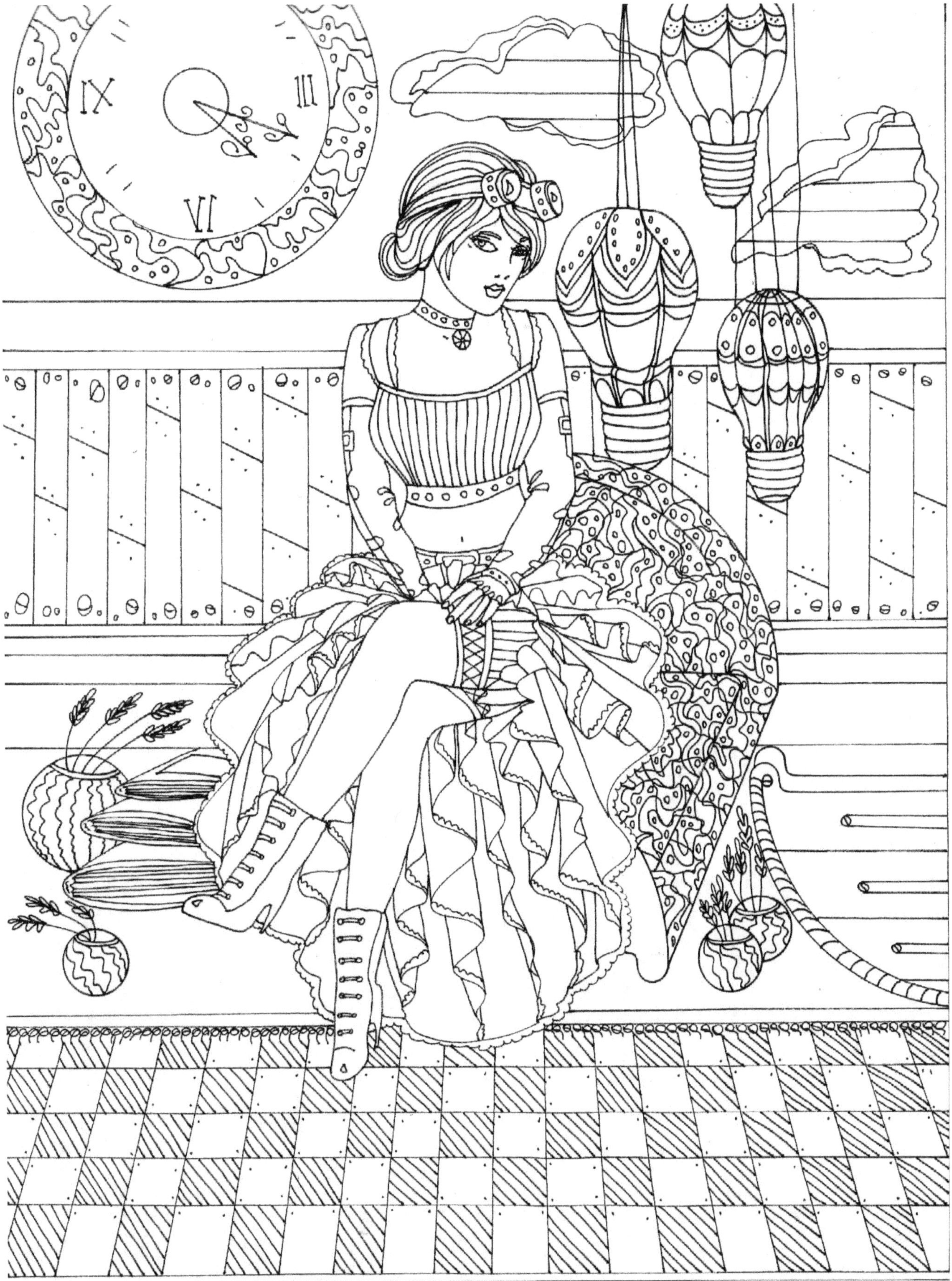
IX
III
VI

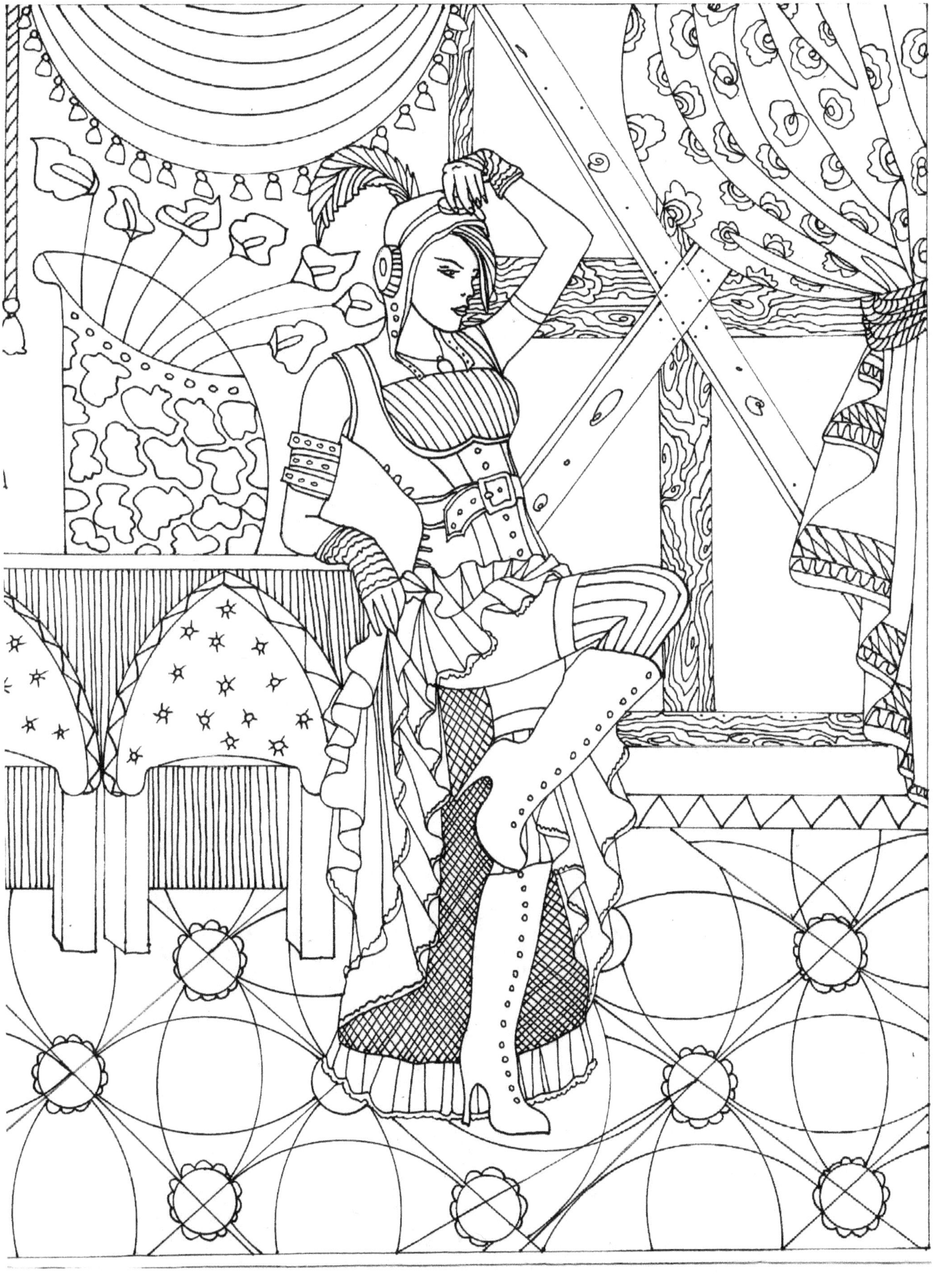

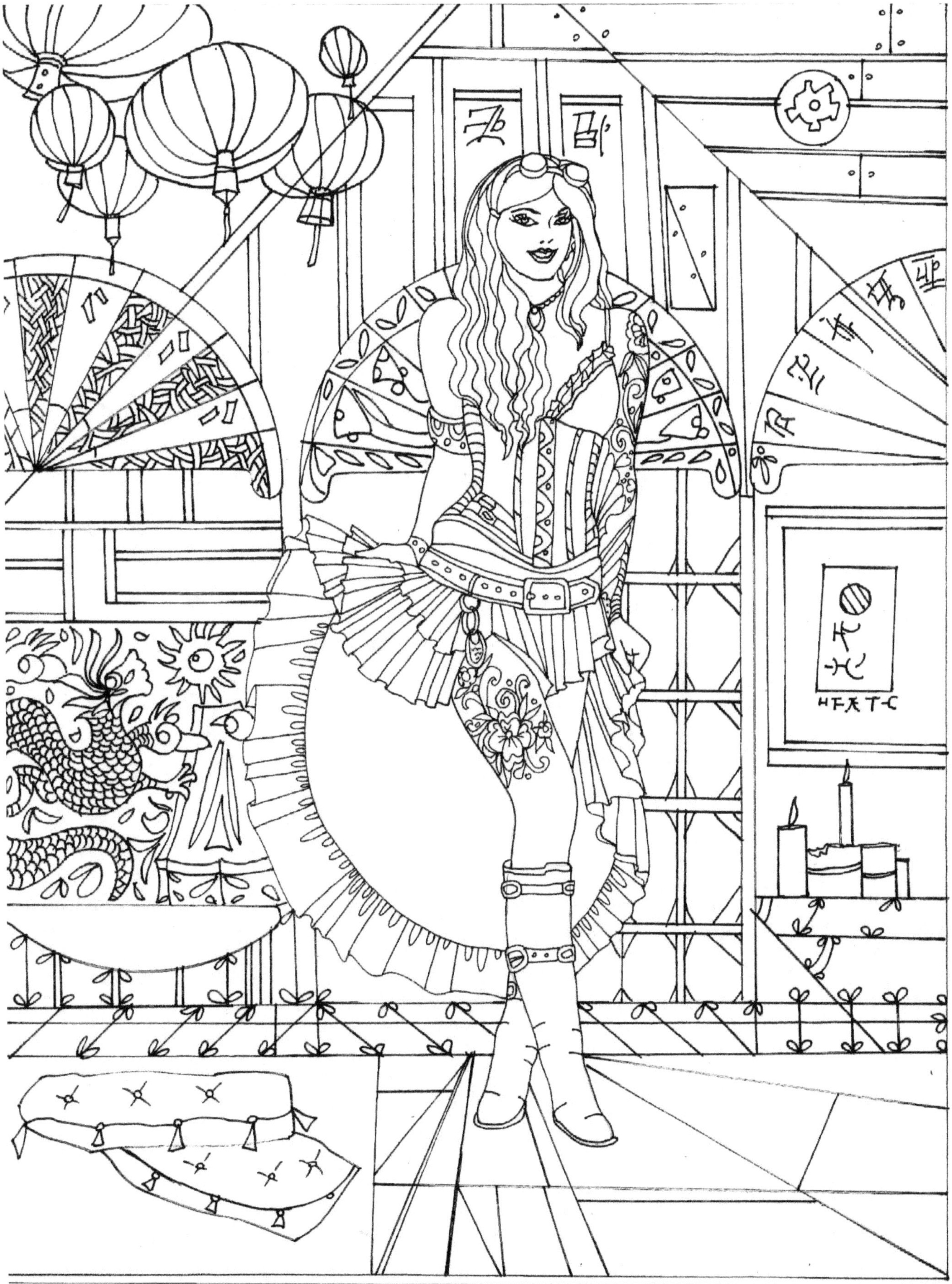

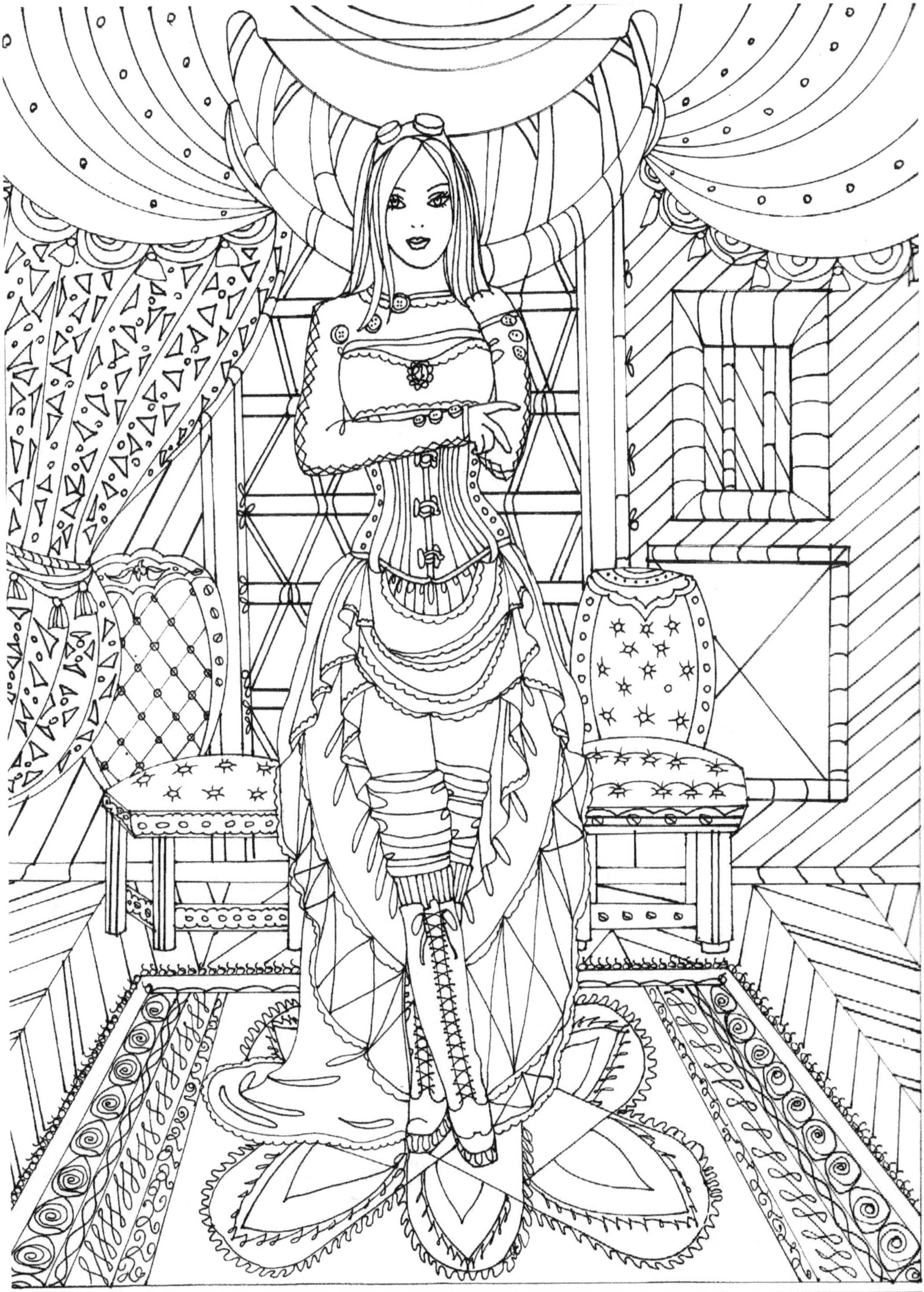

www.ingramcontent.com/pod-product-compliance
Lightning Source LLC
Chambersburg PA
CBHW081241280526
45787CB00006B/2759
9781519513793